ACADEMY OF
LEARNING

Your Complete Preschool Lesson Plan Resource: Volume 5

© **2015 Breely, Crush & Associates, LLC**

Ver. 112214

Table of Contents

Holiday Happenings (continued)

Machines & Tools 43

Fairy Tales in Three's 58

Where To Get What You Need 72

Educator Biography

Sharlit Elliott has a B.S. in Elementary Education and Early Childhood from Brigham Young University and has been a teacher for over 15 years working with children ages 3-5. She keeps current on changes in education by attending University classes and conferences several times a year. Besides having raised five children, she has held various leadership positions with the Girl Scouts and the 4-H program. She enjoys gardening, scrapbooking, reading and of course working with children.

How to Use This Book

This book is designed for a teacher working with children ages 3-5 in a classroom, homeschool or home preschool environment. One of the most important aspects of this series is that it includes fun activities that will enhance their skills. These lessons plans, games and ideas are all for you to use. Don't forget, these are complete lessons and activities that have been designed for compliance with federal and state guidelines for education. We go above and beyond to bring you MORE than what's expected in the public school system.

We will refer to your students as "your children or class". That includes whatever area you are using these lessons for: homeschool or preschool. Our lesson plans include improving student's abilities through activities. The skills we will be working with include: listening skills, music, movement, language and literacy, mathematics, science, fine motor, creative art, sensory, dramatic play, and social skills.

The book is organized by themes which will help you quickly find just the right information. The headings in the book will direct you quickly to large group, small group, and free time activities. It will also provide ideas for field trips.

This book will include the following areas:

Group Activities/Circle Time

- Music & Movement is used to help develop large muscles in arms and legs. These need to be developed before children can be successful in small muscles activities such as used in writing or cutting with scissors. This area also helps children learn to enjoy music and the basics such as beat, loud/soft and fast/slow.

- Language & Literacy is how we help children learn vocabulary, story order, thinking skills, recall, concepts of the theme, and expressive language.

Small Group Activities/Table Times

- Math & Cognitive is used to teach numbers, shapes, patterns, sorting, thinking and reasoning skills.

- Fine Motor Skills develop small muscles to be able to draw, write, manipulate small things, to tear, and to cut with scissors.

- Language & Literacy is used to develop skills such as expressive writing, visual memory, matching letters, letter sounds, categorizing items, directional words, and opposites.

- Other creative activities to develop their own uniqueness as an individual.

Free Time

- Creative arts to draw, build, and develop their imagination.

- Sensory activities are used to learn through exploration and using their senses.

- Dramatic Play & Social Development let children take on different roles, solve problems, find solutions, and develop social interactions.

- Science helps children explore by experimenting, identifying problems, guessing what will happen, checking to see what did happen, questioning how things happened, and developing a plan of what to do next.

- Gross Motor Skills to practice using large and small muscles in fun activities.

- Field Trip Ideas to help children use real places to learn about the world.

Throughout the book we will use the following icons to show the different types of activities:

MUSIC & MOVEMENT

LANGUAGE & LITERACY

MATH & COGNITIVE

FINE MOTOR SKILLS

CREATIVE ARTS

SENSORY

DRAMATIC PLAY & SOCIAL DEVELOPMENT

SCIENCE

GROSS MOTOR SKILLS

FIELD TRIP IDEAS

Introduction to the Units

These lesson plans have been used during the fall with great success. Because of different opinions, policies or religions, sometimes Halloween is not observed in a preschool setting. For example, in the federal Head Start programs, holidays are not observed nor are birthdays. With a mixed group of children, all the lesson plans (except Halloween) can be adjusted, modified or used to replace this particular holiday. In this way, children who do observe the holiday at home are still able to enjoy the "season" and other aspects of the holiday in a fun and safe way. Because all these topics take place in the same season, there is a little overlap from unit to unit, allowing you to pick and choose your favorite activities.

Winter Weather

GROUP ACTIVITIES/CIRCLE TIME

MUSIC AND MOVEMENT

These fun songs are great music and movement activities for winter fun.

"I Like to Play in the Snow" from "I Have a Song For You About Seasons and Holidays" Brite Music Enterprises, Inc.

"Playful Little Jack Frost" from "I Have a Song For You About Seasons and Holidays" Brite Music Enterprises, Inc.

"Mister Wind Is a Mischief" from "I Have a Song For You About People and Nature" Brite Music Enterprises, Inc.

"Dainty Little Snowflakes" from "I Have a Song For You About People and Nature" Brite Music Enterprises, Inc. This is a fun song to pretend that your children are snowflakes and they can dance around to the music.

"The Freeze" from "We All Live Together" Vol. 2 by Greg & Steve CD. This is a fun movement song. Children can pretend to "freeze" (stop whatever they are doing, wherever they are) when the word "freeze" is mentioned in this song and then continue to move again to the music.

"Weather" from "Ole! Ole! Ole!" by Dr. Jean en Español. This song is recorded first in English and then in Spanish.

"The Snowman" from "My Toes Are Starting To Wiggle!" Book and tape by Miss Jackie Silberg.

"Six Little Snowmen" from "My Toes Are Starting To Wiggle!" Book and tape by Miss Jackie Silberg. This is a counting song that the children really love. You can have six of the children at a time be the snowmen in this song and act it out while counting.

"Falling Snow" from Children's Songbook, Published by The Church of Jesus Christ of Latter-day Saints.

"Once There Was a Snowman" from Children's Songbook, Published by The Church of Jesus Christ of Latter-day Saints. This is a fun song where children pretend to be snowmen. When the song says "tall, tall, tall" the children raise their bodies from a stooped potion by raising their bodies as high as possible up on their tip toes. Then when it says "small" they get lower and lower until they are a puddle (laying) on the floor.

LANGUAGE AND LITERACY

Subjects for this unit can include books on weather knowledge, clothing to wear to the winter, and playing in the snow.

Watching the Seasons by Edana Eckart, Scholastic Inc., 2005.

Watching the Weather by Edana Eckart, Scholastic Inc., 2005.

Weather: A First Discovery Book Scholastic Inc., 1991.

Whatever the Weather by Karen Wallace, Eyewitness Readers Level 1, DK Publishing Inc., 1999.

A Letter to Amy by Ezra Jack Keats, Harper & Row, Publishers 1968.

Cloudy With A Chance of Meatballs by Judi Barrett, Scholastic Inc., 1993.

It Looked Like Spilt Milk by Charles G. Shaw, Scholastic Inc., 1989.

Frosty the Snowman by Steve Nelson and Jack Rollins, Scholastic Inc., 2004.

A Hat for Minerva Louise by Janet Morgan Stoeke, Scholastic Inc., 1996.

Five Little Penguins Slipping On The Ice by Steve Metzger, Scholastic Inc., 2002.

The Big Snow by Berta and Elmer Hader, Scholastic Inc., 1990.

When Winter Comes by Robert Maass, Scholastic Inc., 1996.

Snowballs by Lois Ehlert, Scholastic Inc., 1997.

The Little Match Girl by Hans Christian Andersen, G.P. Putnam's Sons, 1990.

Sadie and the Snowman by Allen Morgan, Scholastic Inc., 1987.

Mrs. Toggle's Zipper by Robin Pulver, Scholastic Inc., 1993.

Six Snowy Sheep by Judith Ross Enderle and Stephanie Gordon Tessler, Scholastic Inc., 1994.

A Very Merry Snowman by Joanne Barkan, Scholastic Inc., 1992.

Boots by Anne Schreiber, Scholastic Inc., 1994.

Geraldine's Big Snow by Holly Keller, Greenwillow Books, 1988.

Happy Winter by Karen Gundersheimer, Harper & Row, Publishers, 1982.

Penguin Pete and Pat by Marcus Pfister, Scholastic Inc., 1989.

Frozen Noses by Jan Carr, Scholastic Inc., 2001.

The Wild Toboggan Ride by Suzan Reid and Eugenie Fernandes, Scholastic Inc., 1992.

Copy Me, Copycub by Richard Edwards, Scholastic Inc., 1999.

Flip and Flop by Dawn Apperley, Scholastic Inc., 2002.

White Snow Bright Snow by Alvin Tresselt, Scholastic Inc., 1988.

Little Polar Bear and the Husky Pup by Hans de Beer, Scholastic Inc., 2000.

The Snowy Day by Ezra Jack Keats, Scholastic Inc., 1987.

The Missing Mitten by Steven Kellogg, Scholastic Inc., 2002.

The Mitten by Jan Brett, Scholastic Inc., 1990.

Froggy Gets Dressed by Jonathan London, Scholastic Inc., 1995.

Don't forget to always have a discussion after reading each book. Ask mostly open ended questions and sometimes have the children look for different things while they listen to the story.

An example of how to do this is as follows: before reading Froggy Gets Dressed, ask the children to look for all the different things that Foggy put on before going outside in the snow. Then after reading the story, ask children to tell you the clothing Froggy put on before going outside. Then ask them why do we wear gloves, etc.?

SMALL GROUP ACTIVITIES/TABLE TIMES

MATH & COGNITIVE

Snowman Number Cards

Make ten snowmen, each with a number from 1-10 on them. Make and laminate several sets for use at the table. Place them in a small zip lock bag with a cereal such as Cheerios in it. Create one set for each two children.

Pair up children that need help with a child who recognizes some or most of the numbers. Tell children to take turns with their partner naming the numeral and putting that number of pieces of cereal on each snowman in their set. Observe children and help out as needed for this practice and learning game.

When children are finished, let them have the remaining cereal left in their bag to eat. Have children dump the cereal that they used in the activity in the garbage. If they don't have any cereal left in their bag, give them some to put in their bag.

Winter Number Activity

Prepare a page with number dot tracers, space to write numbers and pictures of winter objects to count. See example Make copies of your pattern for each child to use.

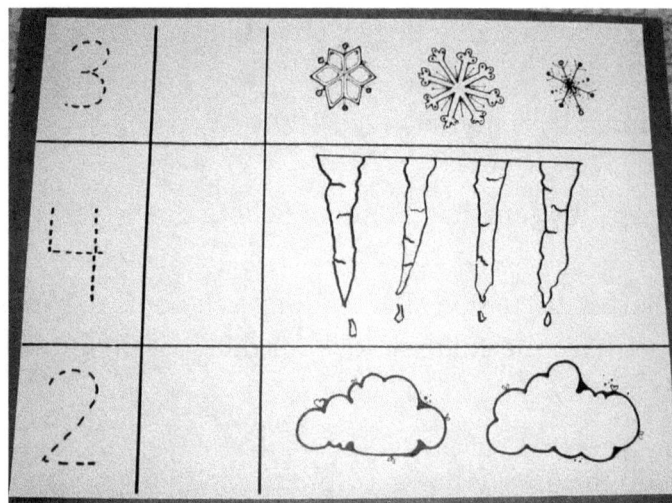

Pass out sheets for each child and pencils. Children will trace numbers and count objects on each roll and then write the number of objects in the blank space.

Snow Hats

Make a snow hat pattern like the example below, with a column for numbers and other columns to put math cubes or other counters in. Then copy your pattern off in different colors. Make four or five hats and then laminate them. Provide twenty math cubes or counters for each card and place them into a small zip lock bag.

Children can put counters in the column next to the numbers one at a time while counting to five. Then they can put the correct number of counters across from each number. Example next to the number three they will put one marker in each column next to the number three until there are three there.

On the last line where there is a question mark children will put one counter in as many columns as they desire beside the "?" mark. Then they will count the number of counters and point to the correct number in the number column. They can take turns doing the "?" mark column with another child or with the teacher.

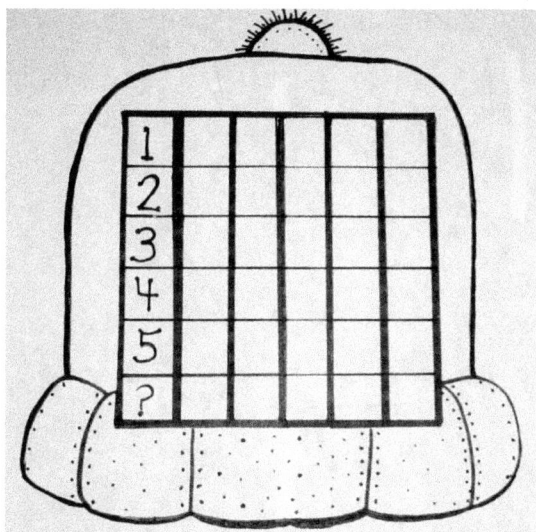

Snowman Match

For this activity you will use the same snowman patterns in the "Snowman Number Cards" activity. This time instead of writing numbers on them use drawings of different shapes and color in the shape on each snowman. Place the shape in the middle ball of each snowman. Each shape needs to have a match. Then laminate them.

Place the snowman cards face up for children to see the shapes. Then point to each shape and have the children say the shape names together. Then the children will take turns picking two snowman cards that match and saying the shape name.

After the children have learned more of the shape names, turn the shape side down on the table. Now use the cards for a memory concentration game. Only let each child pick three cards to try and make memory matches of the same two shapes. If they make a match they will say the name of the two shapes that match and in no matches they will replace the cards back down on the table. The game will continue with the next child taking his or her turn. The play continues until all of cards have been matched.

Match the Mittens

Make a simple mitten pattern such as the one in the example. Now, draw designs on the mittens that are simple, like lines, polka dots, etc. Make eight different designs and then use a copy machine to print them on to different colors of paper. Make two of each design using the same color so that they will match. Children will take turns looking at the different designs and matching them.

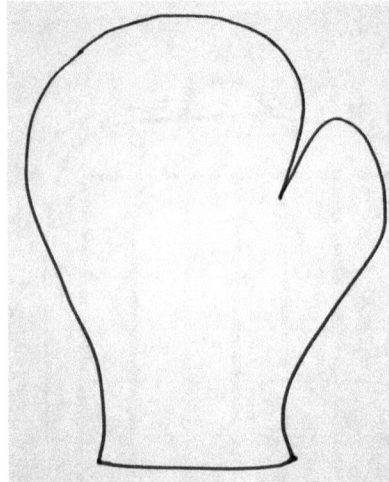

Five Little Snowmen

Make a sled from colored poster board and use snowman pattern from "Snowman Number Cards" to make five snowmen. Laminate these pieces and mount the snowmen on a craft (Popsicle) stick. Children will take turns holding the stick puppet snowmen by the sled which is held by either the teacher or another child. Then children will chant Five Little Snowmen to the turn of "Five Little Monkeys Jumping on the Bed."

The children will act out the song by taking turns pretending that a snowman fell off the sled and lost his head. They will repeat the chorus part - Mama called Frosty and Frosty said, "No more snowmen riding on a sled." Have the rest of the children at the table hold up five fingers to represent the five snowmen and have them put one finger down each time one of the snowmen falls off the sled. See example.

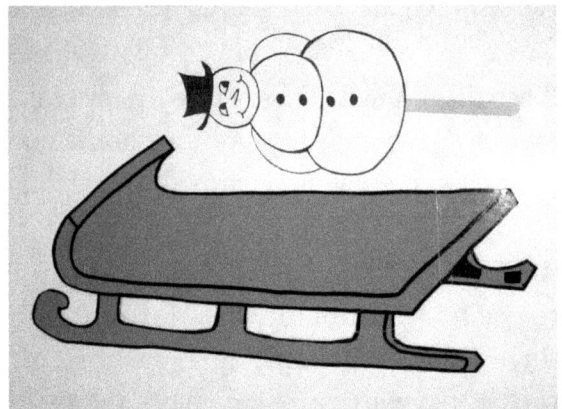

Five Little Snowmen

Five little snowmen riding on a sled.

One fell off and lost his head.

Mama called Frosty and Frosty said,

"No more snowmen riding on a sled."

Four little snowmen riding on a sled.

One fell off and lost his head.

Mama called Frosty and Frosty said,

"No more snowmen riding on a sled."

Three little snowmen riding on a sled.

One fell off and lost his head.

Mama called Frosty and Frosty said,

"No more snowmen riding on a sled."

Two little snowmen riding on a sled.

One fell off and lost his head.

Mama called Frosty and Frosty said,

"No more snowmen riding on a sled."

One little snowman riding on a sled.

He fell off and lost his head.

Mama called Frosty and Frosty said,

"No more snowmen riding on a sled."

And he put all the heads back on the snowmen.

Snowmen Sizes

Children will use white play dough to make four different sizes of snowmen. Encourage children to make balls of dough to create their snowmen. Children will then place their snowmen in size order from biggest to smallest. Then they will tell the teacher which snowman is the largest and which is the smallest.

14

Self-Hardening Play Dough

4 cups flour	1 tsp. alum
1-1/2 cups salt	

Mix the flour, salt and alum together. Then add the water to it gradually.

Stir to form a ball in bowl. Add more water it won't Hold together. Next knead dough. Place in a sealed container until ready to use. After shapes have been Made leave to dry. All these ingredients can be found in the baking/spice aisle of the grocery store.

FINE MOTOR SKILLS

Snow Flakes

Teacher will demonstrate folding and cutting a snowflake. Use white copy paper for this activity because thick paper like cardstock or construction paper would be hard for the children to cut through. Give each child a piece of paper and a pair of scissors. Children will follow your demonstrations by doing each of the steps with you one at a time.

Children will fold their paper in half, then in half again and then fold paper to side to side forming a triangle with the folded edges together. Then cut off the extra paper that is left over along the triangle edge. Now have them cut small triangles and other small shapes on the edges of the triangle. Be careful not to connect the cut shapes too close or the snowflake will not hold together. Now unfold and enjoy hanging the pretty snowflakes from the classroom ceiling.

Sponge Paint Flakes

Go to a craft store to buy sponges in snowflake shapes or make your own sponge snowflakes by buying thin sponges and cutting them into simple snowflakes. Prepare white poster paint by mixing a little liquid dish soap into the paint. This makes it so it will wash out of the children's clothes easier if they accidently spill. Provide blue paper for each child.

Children will dip their sponges into the paint and then stamp it onto the blue paper to form snowflakes in the blue sky.

An optional addition would be to have children sprinkle clear or silver glitter on the paint while it is still wet. Then when it's dry it will sparkle. See example.

Swab Snowflakes

For this activity you will need plastic lids from small containers. Make sure you start saving early so that you have one for each child. You can also ask parents to save clean lids for you, such as ones found on margarine. Buy plastic cotton swabs (Q-tips) and cut them in half. You will also need glue bottles and glitter.

Children will fill their lid with about ¼ - ½ inch of glue. Then they will arrange the swabs in a circle with all the plastic ends meeting in the center of the circle. Next have them sprinkle glitter over the glue and let it dry. When it is dry it will peel out of the lid and the glue will hold the snowflake together. You can hang it by punching a hole in the hardened glue and attach it with yarn. See example.

Mitten Lacing

First you will need to prepare a large pattern such as in the example. Now put the pattern on top of colored sheets of construction paper and cut around the mitten pattern. Continue making mittens until you have made two - a top and a bottom, for each child in the class. Then put the two mittens together with a paper clip and use a hand held paper punch to punch holes (circles) around the edges of the mitten leaving the part where your hand would go in free of punches.

Prepare the yarn for the children to sew around the edges by taping the ends of the yarn or by placing the ends in glue and leaving them to dry. The edges of the yarn need to be stiff so the children can get the yarn through the holes. Leave the mittens paper clipped together until the mittens have been sewn together to make it easier for the children.

Demonstrate how to weave in and out of the holes to sew the mitten together. Now the children will sew their mitten together.

Mitten Collage

Use the same pattern as in "Mitten Lacing" to make a mitten (or two for a pair) of mittens for each child in the class. You can use whatever color you would like to cut the mittens from. Prepare a supply of collage items such as colored noodles, sequins, small foam shapes, beans or whatever you have to work with that can decorate their mittens.

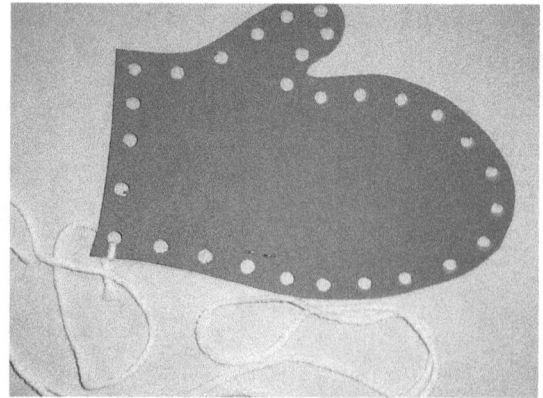

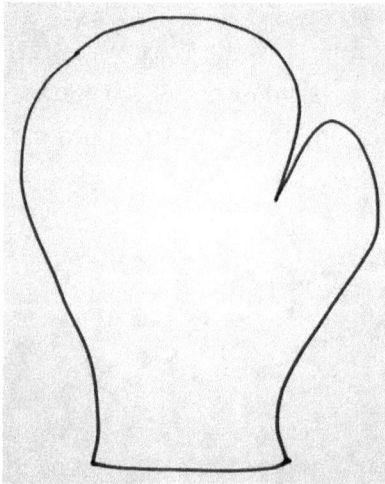

Children will each be given a mitten, small bottle of glue and the collage material to decorate their mitten. Let them decorate it any way that they want. Encourage them to put each piece of collage on one at a time, because the handling of the small items helps them to develop their finger strength and dexterity.

If they have made a pair of mittens, then have them punch a hole on the side that the hand goes through to hook the pair together with a piece of yarn. The pair can be hung in the center of the yarn will hang down like real mittens that are thread through coat sleeves. They look cute that way, but it's not necessary to make two of them if you are short of time or resources. See example.

Snowman

Create a snowman pattern by using different sizes of plastic lids. The biggest lid being the bottom. The smallest the top and middle size one will be the middle. Trace around theses shapes by over lapping the circle to form the body of the snowman. Then cut out the snowman using the outside lines of the lids. Now cut out five or six snowman patterns to be used as tracers at your table. See example.

Then draw a hat pattern for the snow man and cut out enough hats for each child in your class. Also cut out stripes

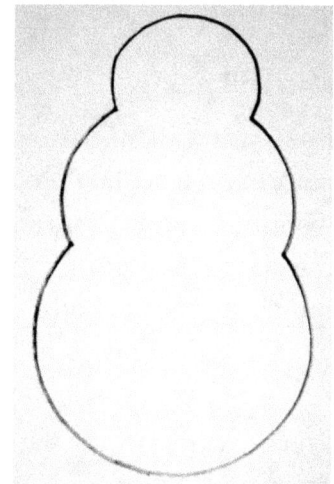

of patterned paper for them to use for scarves. They could also cut out their own hat. See Hat and scarf examples.

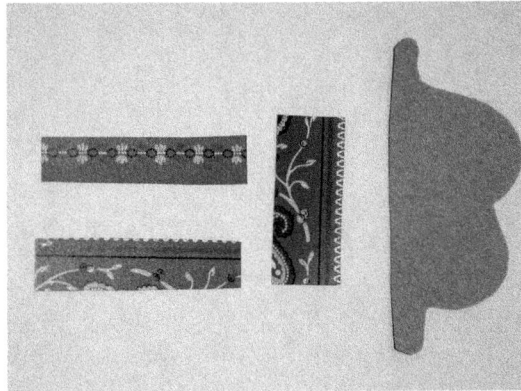

Children will use tracers to make the snowman body. They will then cut out their snowman and glue on the scarf and hat. Next, they will draw or use glue with plastic wiggly eyes. For the buttons, use real buttons or children can drawn their own. Be sure that the markers are set out so that children are free to draw details like eyelashes, noses and mouths.

Snow Tree

Draw and cut out a simple tree trunk from brown construction paper for each child in the class. See example.

Also cut small squares from sponge to represent snowflakes. The sponges should then be glued onto the ends of empty film containers or empty spools of thread to make them "stampers" and easy to hold and work with.

Mix one half part white poster paint with one part white glue and two parts shaving cream together. Place this mixture in a thin layer on foam trays.

Children will glue their tree trunk to a piece of light blue paper in either direction on their paper. Then children will use the sponge holders to dip into the paint, cream and glue mixture and press the mixture lightly over the tree to create snow. They can also add snow to the ground. This snow will be a dimensional snow on their paper. It will dry as a dimensional snow too.

LANGUAGE AND LITERACY

Season Clothing

Bring seasonal clothing articles from home such as swim suits, shorts, sleeveless tops, sandals, coats, boots, sweaters, warm pants and long sleeve shirts. Have the children talk about each piece of clothing and tell what time of the year or what season you would wear each article. Make sure that all the children have a turn discussing the clothing. Then have them sort the clothing in warm weather and cool weather clothing. Talk about seasons with the children and show pictures from one of the books showing seasons.

Another day, have the children fold a piece of paper in half and have them draw pictures of themselves wearing different clothing for cool weather on one side of the page and warm weather clothing on the other half of the page. Also, have them dictate the names of the clothing that they are wearing to you or something they want to share about their picture. Write their words on the page.

Snowflake Positions

Make five or six snowflakes and laminate them. Each child will be given a snowflake to put in various positions that the teacher says, such as: place the snowflake on your nose, under your chair, over your head, between the bend of your arm, in your hand behind your back. Children will say the positions aloud as a class while they put the snowflake in the correct spot. Then they will take turns being the leader and telling others where to put their snowflake while they put their own snowflake in the correct position.

Snowman Match Cards

Make a pattern of six slightly different snowmen such as in the example.

Use a copy machine to copy these snowmen, so they will have exact matches. Now mount four different snowmen on a card. This will be each child's game board. Next make a different variation on the next card and continue to make cards in this manner until you have five or six cards and then laminate them.

Copy the snowmen patterns until you have enough of them to be able to match each of the snowmen cards. Mount the cards, laminate them, and cut them apart.

To play the game, give each child a game board and place all the separate game cards face up in the center of the table. Children will take turns looking closely at the cards to find a match for their game card when it is their turn. Then when it is their turn they will place a matching card on their game board.

Teachers make sure that the cards really match and point out the differences when they do not match. Then the next player will take a turn finding a matching card. Be sure and ask children how the card they picked is the same or if not the same, in what way it is different than the card they choose. Play continues until everyone has filled their cards with matching cards.

It Looked Like Spilt Milk

Read the book It Looked Like Spilt Milk to the children. After you have read the book, give and each child a paper with markers, chalk or crayons to draw their cloud shape. After the children draw their shape, they will tell the teacher about their picture and the teacher will write their words about their picture. If the children just say a few words, expand on their words by repeating what the child said giving them a chance to elaborate. Then repeat what they said to make sure you have it correctly and add a word or two to describe it if necessary.

Now have them say the whole part together. Example - Child says "It's an ice cream". Teacher says "It's an ice cream that is _____." Child says "pink" Then teacher says, "It's an ice cream that is pink and tastes like _____." Child and teacher continue on in this same manner until the child has expanded his words into a short paragraph about their picture.

The Mitten

The teacher will retell the story of The Mitten using pictures of the animals in the order that they went into the mitten in the story. Then children will take turns retelling the story using the pictures the teacher used to tell it. Then they will take turns telling you their favorite part of the story. They will also tell you why they liked that part.

If possible, copy the animal pictures from coloring pictures and shrink them using the copy machine, so that they will be small enough to fit into a paper mitten. Make each child a mitten to place their animals in. Then they could use their own pictures when retelling the story to the children at the table. Next, have the children take their mitten story home with a note to their parents asking them to listen to their child's story of The Mitten.

Color Snowmen

Purchase the flannel color snowmen set from online at http://www.storytimefelts.com/catalog/index.php or make your own snowmen wearing different colored hats with matching scarves on poster board. Use the snowman shapes from "Snowman Game Cards" as an example of how to make them, but add different colored hats and a matching colored scarf to them. Laminate the snowmen to make them more durable. Then spread the snowmen on the table and have children take turns to choose a snowman and tell the color of its hat and matching scarf.

Play the game again but this time, have the children pick a snowman and find a matching color of the hat and scarf. When they find their matching pieces, have them show them to the other children and say the color name. Continue playing with another child choosing another snowman and find the matching color, showing it and naming colors. Continue in this manner until everyone has had at least one turn.

First Letter Name Sounds

Prepare a picture of a penguin for each child with the beginning letter of their first name written large with white chalk and the rest of their name written in smaller letters with a different color of chalk such as light blue.

Children will each be given their penguin with their first letter written on it and asked one at a time, if they know what letter it is. Then as a class, say the letter name aloud together. The teacher will lead them in making the letter sound. Then, the next child will hold up their penguin and say (with help) the letter name and make the letter sound. Continue until everyone has had a turn. If some of the first letters in your group are the same as another child, ask if they know whose name had the same first letter. Then go through all the names and letter sounds one more time with each child holding up his penguin when it's their turn. See example.

FREE TIME

CREATIVE ARTS

Cut out large mittens and place them on the easel with water colors. Children can choose to connect two mittens together with yarn for a set or just do one mitten. See example.

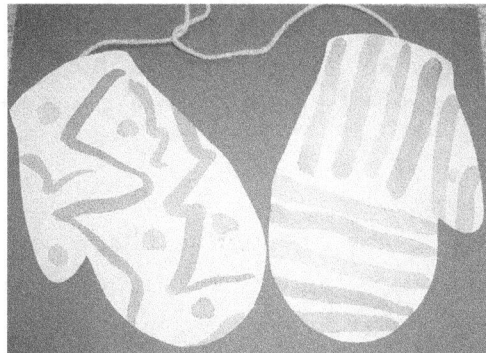

Another day on the easel, have white paper and show children how to use pastels (chalk) on their side to make soft colors. Then show them how they can make the colors softer by rubbing them. Let them experiment with the colors and rubbings.

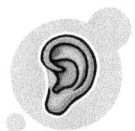

SENSORY

Place real snow in a pail and place it in the sensory table. If real isn't available you can get

"Insta-Snow In A Jar" a substance that looks like and feels like snow. It expands and becomes cold when water has been added to it. You can purchase it from school supply stores such as Constructive Playthings at www.cptoys.com or many other places online.

DRAMATIC PLAY & SOCIAL DEVELOPMENT

Winter Camping

For this activity, have parents help you out by donating things that would be used while camping in the cold weather. Some of the items could be flannel shirts, hunting hats, boots, a small tent or a card table for a tent with a sheet over it, a cooler, old pans and dishes, flash lights, old cameras, old sleeping bags and pretend foods. You can save empty food boxes use as muffin mixes and use them for pretend foods. Also empty cans that have been washed and have duct tape put over the sharp edges make great pretend food.

Have the tent set up with the sleeping bags and the other equipment for the children to enjoy a lot of fun pretending and sharing with each other. Be sure and set up rules for the tent and other items before having children use them, so that they can all be treated fairly.

SCIENCE

Freeze several large cans or containers of ice for the science table. Prepare them with plenty of time for them to freeze all the way through before the time that they will be needed. Talk about frost with the children and tell them that our class can make its own frost. Then bring out the can of ice and leave it on the table. Have the children check back on it in a little while to see if there are any changes. After they have all had a chance to see it, let them touch it and try scratching some it off. Ask children how they think that the frost got there and what will happen to it during the day. Have children observe it during the day and help them to understand what is happening.

When that can has melted around the edges, put the remaining ice in a bowl. Ask why is it melting? Then put rock or regular salt and have them sprinkle some on the ice on one side of the ice. Ask children to guess what may happen to the ice with the salt on it and to the side that doesn't have ice on it. Have them observe both sides during the day and see what happens to both sides. Discuss what the children saw before going home. Have science books from the library on the science table that show and talk about frost, ice, snow and hail.

GROSS MOTOR SKILLS

Remind parents that you will be going outside on winter days and to have them dress their children appropriately for the cold weather. When the snow is fresh, tell the children that they will be going outside and to get all their special warm clothing on. Have them go to the circle when they are ready. Then give instruction to the children about your safety rules. Then tell them that they will be following in your footsteps like in follow the leader. Lead the children around the yard while they walk in your footprints. Next tell them to play in the snow and make their own footprint trails.

On other days, help the children build snowmen and other snow things. Also have a place for children to throw snowballs at a target so other children won't be their target. The corners of the yard could have boxes for targets with pictures of snow animals on them such as a large bear or something as simple as an X fastened on to the back side of it. Make sure if you use pictures that they have been laminated to protect them from the wet snow or draw simple ones that you don't care if they get ruined.

It is also fun for children to shovel snow from the sidewalks. You can go to stores such as Home Depot to buy shovels with adjustable handles that are used to keep in car trunks to dig cars out. With the handles shortened they are just right for children's use.

Provide small spray bottles with trigger handles to use for spraying colored water. Let the children spray the snow. You soon will have a colorful play ground. Be sure and let children know that they can only spray the snow and that they must take turns so that others can have fun too. This is a great activity that builds a lot of finger strength.

FIELD TRIP IDEAS

Make arrangements with parents to accompany your class on a snow sledding trip. Pick a place before the date that won't be crowded and has a gentle hill with snow on it. Have permission notes from the parents and have a safe way to travel there. Plan ahead to obtain as many sleds as possible so that the children don't have to wait too long for a turn. I usually have six of the long toboggan type sleds that two children can ride on at a time. Adjust your numbers of sleds depending on the number of children in your class.

Also, let parents know that on this special day they need to be to school on time to take their children home.

Make sure you go over safety rules with the adults and children before going on your field trip. Have the adults help you enforce the safety rules. Then be prepared for lots of fun! It is also fun to take hot chocolate and donuts with you when children and adults get a little cold and hungry. Be sure and give children a warning before it's time for them to leave, so they can be prepared to leave. When the children get back to school, have parents take them home to change into their warm and dry clothing.

Holiday Happenings

GROUP ACTIVITIES/CIRCLE TIME

MUSIC AND MOVEMENT

"The Very Best Part of Christmas" from "I Have A Song For You About Seasons and Holidays" Brite Music Enterprises, Inc.

"Must Be Santa" from "Singable Songs" by Raffi. For this song, find pictures from Christmas coloring books and copy them to go with the words in the song. This will make it easier for the children to learn the words of the song. Examples of the pictures you would use are - Santa with a long white beard, Santa's boots, his suit, and his cap.

"My Dreydel" from "Singable Songs" by Raffi.

"Here's Our Little Pine Tree" by Miss Jackie Silberg, from book/tape My Toes Are Starting To Wiggle!

"Nine Little Reindeer" by Miss Jackie Silberg, from book/tape My Toes Are Starting To Wiggle!

"We Wish You A Merry Christmas" by unknown from Miss Jackie Silberg, book/tape My Toes Are Starting To Wiggle!

"Jingle Bells" from Southern Country Christmas Favorites CD, KRB Music Companies. Brentwood, TN 37027 (or choose your own variation).

"Santa Claus Is Coming To Town" from Southern Country Christmas Favorites CD, KRB Music Companies (or choose your own variation).

"Frosty The Snowman" from Southern Country Christmas Favorites CD, KRB Music Companies (or choose your own variation).

"Deck The Halls" from Southern Country Christmas Favorites CD, KRB Music Companies (or choose your own variation).

"Rudolph The Red Nosed Reindeer" from Southern Country Christmas Favorites CD, KRB Music Companies (or choose your own variation).

"We Wish You A Merry Christmas" from Southern Country Christmas Favorites CD, KRB Music Companies (or choose your own variation).

"White Christmas" from Southern Country Christmas Favorites CD, KRB Music Companies (or choose your own variation).

"Away In A Manager" from Southern Country Christmas Favorites CD, KRB Music Companies (or choose your own variation).

"Jolly Old St. Nick" from Southern Country Christmas Favorites CD, KRB Music Companies (or choose your own variation).

"Spin, Dreydel, Spin" from Macmillian Sing & Learn Program by Newbridge Communications, Inc.

"Santa's Coming" from Macmillian Sing & Learn Program by Newbridge Communications, Inc.

"Building a Snowman" from Macmillian Sing & Learn Program by Newbridge Communications, Inc.

"Freeze and Melt" from Macmillian Sing & Learn Program by Newbridge Communications, Inc.

"Snowflakes" from Macmillian Sing & Learn Program by Newbridge Communications, Inc.

"Santa's Pack" from Macmillian Sing & Learn Program by Newbridge Communications, Inc.

"Red" from Macmillian Sing & Learn Program by Newbridge Communications, Inc.

"My Favorite Color" from Macmillian Sing & Learn Program by Newbridge Communications, Inc.

Teachers, choose how you want to teach holidays and then pick the songs that go along with what you think is best for your class. You might want to have a "Red Day" and then a "Green Day". Other possibilities would be a "Santa week", a "Gingerbread Man" Theme, "A Nutcracker Theme" or a special day for The Polar Express. If you and your parents feel comfortable with religion celebrations, you could have different parents come in to class and celebrate some of their family traditions with the class. All of these activities can be adapted for Christian, Jewish, non-denominational holiday celebrations. If you do not want to or cannot celebrate "Christmas" then you can still celebrate the season by doing "Red Day," "Green Day," etc.

LANGUAGE AND LITERACY

The Joys of Christmas by Kathryn Jackson, Golden Press Western Publishing Company, Inc.

The Golden Christmas Treasury compiled by Rick Bunsen, A Golden Book, Western Publishing Company, Inc.

Christmas Carols Songbook Illustrated by Anne Sikorski, Modern Publishing, A Division of Unisystems, Inc.

Santa's Puzzle Bag by Edward Roberts, Scholastic Inc.

A Surprise For Santa by Florence Parry Heide, The Saalfield Publishing Company.

Rudolph The Red-Nosed Reindeer told by Eileen Daly, A Whitman Book, Western Publishing Company, Inc.

The Night Before Christmas by Clement C. Moore, Modern Publishing, A Division of Unisystems, Inc.

Santa's Surprise Book by Joan Potter Elwart, Golden Press, Western Publishing Company, Inc.

Merry Christmas Mom and Dad by Mercer Mayer, Golden Press, Western Publishing Company, Inc.

Troll's Twelve Months of Christmas by Jill Wolf, Antioch Publishing Company.

Santa's Favorite Story by Hisako Aoki, Ivan Gantschev, Scholastic, Inc.

Noni The Christmas Reindeer by Daphne Doward Hogstrorm, Rand McNally & Company.

Jingle Bells A new story by Kathleen N. Daly, A Golden Book, Western Publishing Company, Inc.

How Spider Saved Christmas by Robert Kraus, Scholastic Book Services.

Claude The Dog A Christmas Story by Dick Gackenbach, Weekly Reader Books Edition, A Clarion Book. This is a great book about sharing and reminds us all to be thankful for our homes.

The Littlest Christmas Tree by Janie Jasin, Book Peddlers, Minnetonka, MN. This book inspires people to hope and appreciate the possibilities of life. It speaks about the Master Creator who made all the trees and children in the world.

The Polar Express by Chris Van Allsburg, Scholastic, Inc. This book is a magical train ride on Christmas Eve that takes a boy to the North Pole to receive a special gift from Santa Claus.

Nutcracker Noel by Kate McMullan, Scholastic, Inc.

The Nutcracker A Christmas Pop-up The Landoll Inc. Ashland, Ohio 1995.

A Christmas Carol A Christmas Pop-up The Landoll Inc. Ashland, Ohio 1995.

The First Christmas A Christmas Pop-up The Landoll Inc. Ashland, Ohio 1995.

Over the River and Through the Wood by Lydia Maria Child, Scholastic, Inc.

Froggy's Best Christmas by Jonathan London, Scholastic, Inc. This book teaches that Christmas is about friends and family too. It also teaches to do your best and that it's okay to make mistakes.

The Little Christmas Tree by Karl Ruhmann, Scholastic, Inc. This story teaches that little trees and children are special no matter what their size.

The Gingerbread Man Illustrated by Irana Shepherd, Price/Stern/Sloan Publishers.

The Gingerbread Boy retold by Dandi, The Landoll Inc.

Buddy's Favorite Christmas Stories and Poems by the Staff of Weekly Reader, Weekly Reader Books.

Enjoy these books and add any of your favorite Christmas stories to teach the children what you feel is important for them at this special time of year.

SMALL GROUP ACTIVITIES/TABLE TIMES

MATH & COGNITIVE

Christmas Card Count

Collect used Christmas cards and ask parents to have their child send in any old Christmas cards for the class to use at school. The teacher will sort out the cards into different lunch bags using different amounts of cards in most bags.

At the table each child will receive a lunch bag with cards in it to count. They will take turns counting the cards in their lunch bags. Then children will trade bags and count the cards in their new bags. After each child counts their cards in the second bag, the teacher will write the number that was in that bag on a piece of paper and put it by the bag counted.

After all the bags have been counted and the number written by each bag, children will take turns saying one of the numbers written. If they child does not know the number by that bag, then he/she opens the bag and counts the cards. Play continues until all the children have had a turn. Play this game again another day.

Candy Jar

For this activity you will need to get a small clear glass jar and put ten pieces of real or fake candy into it. Small erasers often are found at the Dollar store for purchase. Those that look like pieces of candy work well for this activity. Children will come to the table and take turns guessing how many pieces of "candy" are in the jar without counting them.

Teacher will write down each guess number. Then the teacher will take the candy out of the jar and have the children count how many pieces were in the jar. Now the teacher will take the candy and have the children close their eyes while she puts a different amount in the jar. Never put more in the jar than the children can count correctly.

Now proceed to have them open their eyes and take turns guessing again. Proceed as before with recording their guesses and then counting them together. Estimations are an important math skill to learn. At the end of the game you can choose to give them each one piece of the candy or not if you are using "fake" candy.

Writing Numbers

Prepare numerals 1, 2, and 3 for children to trace over or buy wipe off numerals at the store. These numerals should be written three or four times each to a page. They can be bought at a Dollar store or a school supply store. Demonstrate how to trace the numbers by starting at the top and going down. Then have the children trace their numbers. Watch to make sure that they start from the top each time and are trying to stay on the lines. Add more numbers when children know and can write 1, 2, & 3 easily.

Tree Sizes

Make an evergreen tree pattern and then use a copy machine to enlarge or decrease the size of the tree into four distinct sizes. Make a set for each child to use at the table. Then, color the trees green or copy them on green paper and laminate them.

Children will arrange the trees in order from either smallest to biggest or biggest to smallest. Then they will tell you with their own words the size order of their trees. See example.

Toy Bag Counting

For this activity, collect many small toys. You could use items like the toys you get from fast food children's meal bags, small toys from the room and or small toys from the Dollar store. Then put some of the toys into a small bag. Children will take turns taking the toys out.

When all the toys are out of the bag, count them together. Next, have them close their eyes while you put the toys back and either add more or take out some. Be sure to keep the other toys out of view. Children will open their eyes and take turns taking them out again.

Now the children will take turns counting the toys from the bag. After they have counted the toys they get a turn putting the toys in the bag for the next child to count. Limit the number between 1 and 10. The game continues in this manner until all the children have had a turn.

Tree Ornament Count

Prepare ten Christmas trees by drawing, coloring or copying them on green paper. Write the numerals 1-10, one number per tree and then laminate them. Next you will need a small bag of colored "O's" cereal and a box of snack sized plastic bags. Place cereal into the small bags, one for each child.

Children at the table will each be given a tree with a number on it and a bag of cereal. Tell them not to eat the cereal because it won't be clean when others have handled it. Children will take turns saying the number on their tree and watching and listening while the other children say their number.

Then they will place the correct number of ornaments (the O's) on their tree. If some children need help, then hold up one finger at a time and have them help you count until you have reached the number on their tree. Then keep your fingers up until they have put the correct ornaments on their tree.

When they have completed their tree, give them another tree to work on. There is no need to wait for the other children, as long as they have counted correctly. Play continues until they have counted at least three trees. Then give them each a small handful of the clean cereal to eat. Use example from Tree Sizes.

Gingerbread Counters

Draw ten medium sized gingerbread figures and copy them on light tan paper. Next cut them out and laminate them. See example. Buy small candy shaped erasers at a story like Party-Land, Oriental Trading or your local discount store. Buy at least ten for each child that will be at your table at the same time. Buy more if the children can count higher and make the patterns larger if using more candies so that they will fit on to the shape. Use small plastic bags and put ten candy erasers in each bag or more.

Children will decide how many from their bag to put on their gingerbread shape. Then they will count them buy touching each candy eraser one at a time with the teacher or with another child. One child that has no trouble counting could be paired with a child that needs help.

Then the teacher or other child will count them back while they are put back in the bag. Now the teacher or child takes a turn putting the candies on and counting them. Children will count at least three times before leaving the table.

Gingerbread Man

Children will follow the recipe to make gingerbread dough. They will look at the numbers in the recipe and count the amounts of the ingredients they need to measure. After making the dough, they will roll it out and use gingerbread cookie cutters the cut out their gingerbread man. They will also add candy or raisins to make their eyes and buttons. Have the children count their candy or raisin pieces. Place them on a cookie sheet to cook. Use masking tape on the cookie sheet to write children's names by their gingerbread man.

Gingerbread Man Recipe

½ cup shortening	½ cup sugar
½ cup dark molasses	¼ cup water
2 ½ cups flour	¾ tsp. salt
½ tsp. soda	¾ tsp. ginger
¼ tsp. nutmeg	1/8 tsp. allspice
Raisins	Small candies

Cream shortening and sugar together. Blend in molasses, water, and flour. Then add salt, soda, ginger, nutmeg and all-spice. Cover; chill 2 to 3 hours (or until next day). Heat oven to 375 degrees. Roll dough 1/4 inch thick on lightly floured table. Cut with gingerbread cutter; place on ungreased baking sheet.

Press rains or small candies for eyes, nose and buttons. Bake 10 to 12 minutes. Immediately remove from cookie sheet. Cool. Makes about 15 4-inch cookies.

FINE MOTOR SKILLS

Sponge Wreath

For this project you will need to buy thin white paper plates. Then ask parents or a helper to help cut a circle out of the middle of the plates. The circles can be traced by using lids from small containers. See example.

Mix green and red poster paint with liquid dish soap. Put green and red paints in different foam trays. Cut small squares from a sponge and use a clothespin to hold sponge squares.

Children will each be given a prepared paper plate and an apron to wear to protect their clothing. Tell the children to dip the sponge into the green paint and then to push lightly down on the plate to make prints. Tell them to continue using the sponge and paint around the plate to make their wreath. Then they will use their index finger to dip into the red paint and then press their finger on wreath to make the berries. They can also sprinkle glitter on the wreath while the paint is wet if you desire. You can also add a real bow or a paper bow to the wreath if you would like.

Lacing Boot

Make a boot pattern and cut it out for tracing. Parents can help by tracing the pattern on construction paper with staples to hold the shapes together while cutting boots out. When you have two boots for each child, paperclip the boots together. Use a hole punch around the edges. Space your holes about 1 to 1 ½ inches apart, but leaving the top free without punches (where your foot would go in).

Cut a long piece of yarn to thread through the holes. First wrap the ends of the yarn with tape or dip them in glue and lay them straight to dry. Be sure and keep the paperclips on the boots until they are laced together. Children can use markers to decorate their boot. See example.

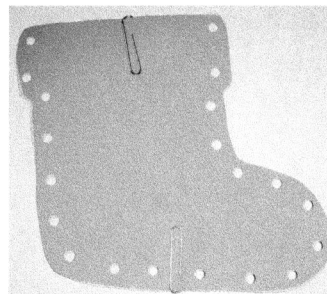

Hand Print Deer Antlers

Help the children trace their hands on tan construction paper. Then the children will cut around the outside outline of their hand. Their hands will be the antlers. Make a 1 ½ inch strip of construction paper to form head band and staple it to form a ring. Now staple the antlers to the band in the front and on either side of the head band. See example. Let children wear these the day you read Rudolph The Red Nosed Reindeer or when you sing the song.

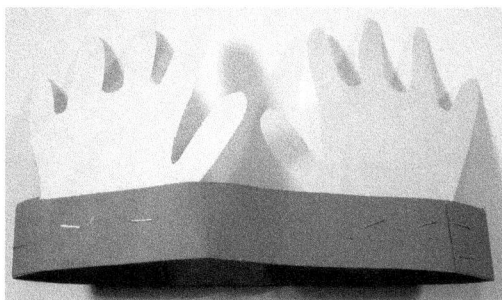

Christmas Trees

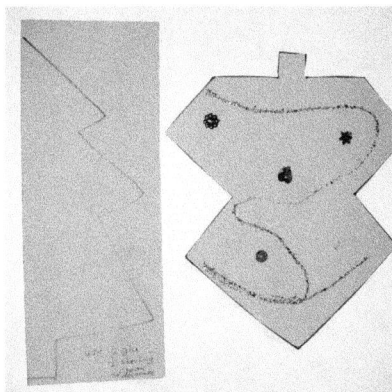

Make a pattern for two different trees using the examples. Trace around the tree shapes on green construction paper. Determine which child will cut out which tree. One tree is easier to cut out than the other one. You will know if the child will need to a challenged to cut the harder one or the easier one. If you have children that all have a difficult time cutting, you may choose to do just one of the trees.

Provide small foam cut out ornaments, noodles, and or stickers to decorate their trees.

Toy Soldier

Use a Christmas coloring book (or go online) to find a picture of a toy soldier. Then use a copy machine to enlarge it to a large size and make copies for each child in your class. See example. Next take five small bottles of glue and put different colors of poster paint in each bottle.

Children will then use different colors of the glue to make thin lines around the toy soldier to decorate it. Let it dry flat so that the colors don't run. This is a fun thing to do after reading The Nutcracker.

Rudolph Head

This is a good activity to do after reading Rudolph the Red-Nosed Reindeer that children will enjoy. Draw a simple deer head, antlers and a bow. Then cut out the antlers and bow. Children will use the pattern deer head to trace around it on brown construction paper and then cut it out. Next they will glue on wiggle eyes, a red pompom nose and cut out the bow. Some children like to glue the bow on the top of the head and some like to put it at the bottom for a bow tie. See example.

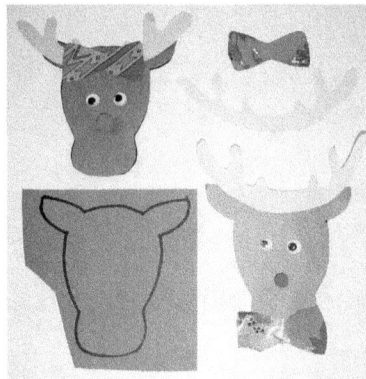

Santa Face

Use a picture from a coloring book or draw your own Santa head. Make copies for each child in your class. Buy inexpensive cotton balls for the beard. Children will take one cotton ball at a time and stretch it out and then glue it onto the picture of Santa's bead. The children continue to pull out cotton balls and glue them on until his beard has been covered. They can also color the face before they start the beard if they want to. See example.

Picture Frame Gift 1

Assemble these items: tongue depressor sticks, glue bottles, individual pictures of the children, white rectangles of poster board, buttons, beads and small Christmas foam shapes.

Children will glue the sticks together as the example shows. Be sure that children's names are written on the back of the frames. Let the frames dry overnight.

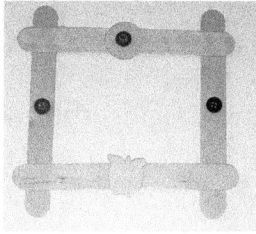

While the frame is drying, children will make wrapping paper for their gift. Put out sheets of large water color paper. Have the children use rubber stamps with red and green ink to decorate the paper. Tell them that this will be their wrapping paper for their present.

The next day the children will decorate the frames using buttons, beads and foam shapes that you have provided for them. Let them glue on their decorations however they choose. After they have dried, place the child's photo behind the frame and tape it to the back. Then add a white square of poster board to the back of the frame to protect the picture. Tape the poster board securely. Now during free play invite the children over one at a time to wrap their special gift with their very own handmade paper. Children will take home their special gift.

Picture Frame 2

The children will not use beads, buttons or foam shapes on the frames this time. Collect small puzzle pieces or buy puzzles at a Thrift store. Then prepare the pieces by spreading them on newspaper and spraying half of the pieces with red paint and the other half with green paint. When the pieces are dry children will make frames as in #1 picture frame. Then when dry they will put pictures in and proceed as in the #1 frame. See example.

Holiday Play dough (Non-Hardening)

2 cups flour
2 cups water
2 Tbs. cooking oil

1 cup salt
2 Tbs. cream of tartar
* red and green food coloring

Combine all the dry ingredients together in a medium sized pan. Add food coloring to the water and mix. Now add the colored water to the dry ingredients and mix well. Cook over low heat, stirring constantly until mixture forms thick clumps around the spoon. Dump onto the counter and let cool slightly. When cool enough to work with, begin kneading (can add optional 4 Tb. of glitter a little at a time). Knead until dough is a mass. Store in a covered container or a plastic bag.

Make red and green colors of dough in separate batches. Provide cookie cutters, rolling pins, plastic knives and scissors for cutting the dough. Tell the children to use one dough color at a time and not mix the two colors together. Let them create whatever they want.

Lacing Gingerbread Men

Buy a half of sheet of a pegboard from a hardware store. Cut the board into pieces about 6 x 10 inches. Next, paint the pegboard pieces a light color. Then trace a gingerbread pattern onto each 6 x 10 piece. Last, paint the gingerbread man with light tan paint and outline it with black paint. Buy long shoe laces at the dollar store to use to lace the gingerbread board. Children at the table can now practice lacing. See example.

LANGUAGE AND LITERACY

Santa Song

Children will learn the song "Santa Bingo" using picture cards. Then children will make their own song cards to take home and sing with their family.

Cut a white poster board into 5 x 5 inch squares and make a set of five for each child. Use a school die cutter (or craft store cutter) to cut the letters S, A, N, T, A. Make a set for each child in the class and also use the die cutter to cut out the open hands and make a set of five hands for each child.

Children will use glue sticks to glue the letters on the back of the individual white square poster boards and the open hand on the other side of the square. Have the children put their song cards in a plastic bag to take home with a copy of the words to the song. Children will love the song and will learn new letter names. See example.

Santa (To the Tune of BINGO)

There is a jolly little man

And Santa is his name oh.

S-A-N-T-A-, S-A-N-T-A, S-A-N-T-A (Point to each letter as you sing it)

And Santa is his name oh!

The next time you sing the song leave out the "S" and instead clap it. As you do this, turn the "S" card over to the hand side. Continue singing the song and leaving out another letter using a clap for the missing letter until all the letters have been turned to claps and you have sung the final line.

Candy Sort

Purchase a bag of snack size M&M candies or Skittles. Each child will be given a small bag to sort into different colors. Children will take turns tell the color names of the candy that they sorted. Then they will put each of their colors in a diagonal line beside each other. They will take turns telling which color was the longest, the shortest and which colors were in between. Then the children can eat them.

Gift Shapes

Prepare large shapes and draw a ribbon and bow on them, so that they will resemble presents. Make the shapes colorful and laminate them. See example.

When children come to your table, ask children one at a time to pick a pretend present and name the shape of it. Then ask the child what they think might be in a present of that size and shape. Accept their answers and have them explain what their reasoning was for why they said that. Have other children give their answers too. Then, have another child pick a present and tell the shape as before and what they think is in that shape present. Continue as before with children contributing their thoughts and thinking on each shape gift.

Christmas Memory Match

For this game you will use index cards and different Christmas stickers. Place one sticker on each card and make a pair of each sticker. When you have made six or seven pairs laminate them. Then, place the cards face down on the table in two lines. Children will play the by taking turns turning over three cards to try and make on match. If they make a match they get to have another turn. When they do not make a match, they put their cards back where they got them and turn them back over. Now the next child takes a turn and play continues until all the cards have been matched up.

Gift of Love

Take a long piece of construction paper and draw lines on it to make a shape of a present with a bow on it. See example. Each child will be given a copy of the drawn present with the words written on it - "My gift of love." The children will be given crayons and markers to draw in the present shape.

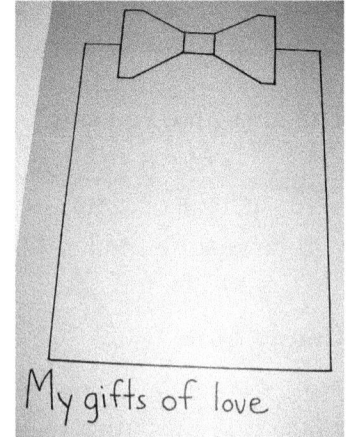

This picture should show different ways that they can serve their family with love. An example would be picking up their toys or helping with a younger sister or brother. You will write their words of love to their families after they have drawn their picture. Children will take the gift home to their family.

Christmas Cards

Set out a selection of used cards that have been collected. Place scissors, paper, markers and glue out for children to use. Children will select from the cards what they would like to use on their own card. Demonstrate how to fold they paper into a half for a large card and fold it in fourths for a small card.

Next the child will cut out the parts of the card they would like to place on their card and glue it down. They may also draw on the card and write simple messages. Have papers with a few greetings printed, so that they can copy the messages on to their cards. Examples would be - "Merry Christmas," Happy Holidays," "I Love my Family." Send the cards home with the children to give to whom they would like.

Holiday Size Order

Use clip art or coloring books to find holiday items such as a star, camel, present, candy cane, toy soldier, gingerbread man, etc. Then use the copy machine to make three or four different items. The items should be about the size of 2 x 2 inches. Now copy each item three times to make a set of three or four different things. Help children learn the meaning of the word "pattern" by show them how to make a two item pattern. Talk about how repeating something in the same way makes a pattern.

Then children will make a two item pattern by repeating the items. Next, talk about making a bigger pattern. Ask the children to see if they can find the repeated items in the pattern. Now have the children make a three piece pattern. Try this again another day and see how much they remember. Then when they can do a three piece pattern correctly, have them work on a four piece pattern.

Gingerbread Man Book

Read to the children the story of the <u>Gingerbread Man</u>. They will also do the math/ cognitive activity of making gingerbread men, but when they are cooked, hide them while they cool. Now announce to the children that the gingerbread men are missing. Tell them to look around the classroom to see if they ran away someplace.

After they have looked around and still haven't found them, invite them to your table and draw on a large gingerbread shaped sheet where they think that the gingerbread man may have gone. After they have drawn their picture, ask them to tell you where they think he is. Write their words on their page.

Put all the pages into a book shaped like a big gingerbread man. A little before it is time to go, read their book to the whole class and be sure and say each child's name on the page that they drew. Now while you are all still sitting together, have someone help you and go over with the child to where you have hidden the gingerbread men. Have the child help you bring them over and say, "Look what I found hiding." Each child receives their cookie to take home or eat then. Keep the completed book in the class where they can look at it and read it. See example of book cover and pages.

CREATIVE ARTS

Make patterns of candy canes, socks, trees and gingerbread men for the easel and put water colors in the trays for them to paint on shapes of poster or butcher paper.

Also, provide red and green poster paint mixed with liquid dish soap and large pieces of water color paper to draw on at the easel. See examples.

SENSORY

Put warm water in the sensory table with a little dish soap for bubbles along with a supply of water toys - such as water wheels with scoops, floating ducks or boats.

Another day, place flour with sifters, pans, bowls, spoons and scoops in the sensory table. They will enjoy stirring the flour and sifting it. They also like to fill the different types of pans and then turn them over like sand pail to create the mold of the pans.

You can also put red or green coloring into water at the sensory table along with a little glitter. Then put in different sizes of clear plastic bottles with funnels and scoops.

DRAMATIC PLAY & SOCIAL DEVELOPMENT

Place dress up clothing along with boy and girl type aprons. Add cooking caps or baking hats, medium sized bowls, spoons (to using for stirring), various baking pans, empty baking boxes, empty milk cartons, empty egg cartons and other empty containers that you have collected. Children will enjoy being the mom/dad or cook/baker.

Another fun dramatic play activity is to create Santa's workshop complete with toys, cash register, pretend money, bags and a supply of pretend paint brushes and pretend machine tools. You could also have an area such as a work bench with wood, craft sticks, markers and glue to create things.

You could also set up an area with dress up clothing, an artificial Christmas tree and a cardboard fireplace. Place dress-up clothing, small toys and Christmas stockings to fill.

SCIENCE

Put different types of lamps with colored light bulbs, flash lights, a small string of Christmas lights and different colored candles (not lit) on the table for children to examine. Also put out colored paddles to look through and shine the different lights through them so children can see the effect.

Demonstrate how fire needs air to burn by lighting one candle and then cover it with a glass bottle so that it won't get air. Talk about what happened to the flame when it was covered. You can also talk briefly about fire safety. Show the children a glow stick and then activate it so that it glows.

A different day, set out a collection of pine cones and pine nuts to sample. Make sure no one is allergic to pine nuts before putting the nuts out to sample. Put out a small collection of different pine needles and books about trees and their cones.

GROSS MOTOR SKILLS

I've Got a Christmas Card

This game is played and sang like "I have a doggie and it won't bite you." Instead of using those words, for this game we'll use these words – "I've got a Christmas card and it's not for you or you, but it's for you."

Children sit in a circle and one child is "it" and that child holds the card in their hand and goes around the circle saying the new words to the song - "I've got a Christmas card and it's not for you or you, but it's for you." The "it" child touches children on the head or shoulder lightly while saying the words.

When the "it" child comes to the child that they want to leave the card with, he says "but it's for you!" and leaves the card with that person and runs around the circle until reaching the place where the child sat and sits in it.

Then when the first child reaches the second child's seat the second child becomes "it." Now the game begins again. Continue playing until each child as had at least one turn.

Musical Chairs

Have each child bring over their chair and place them back to back in the middle of the circle. Then explain the game to the children. Children will walk around the chairs in the circle until the Christmas music stops and then they will hurry over to find a chair to sit on.

The first child to sit down will be able to tell the children how to go around the chairs when the music starts. This child can choose between - skipping around, hopping around, galloping around, tip toeing around or walk around. Play continues for about 15 minutes or until the children are starting to get restless.

FIELD TRIP IDEAS

Make arrangements to visit a mall to see all the Christmas decorations and Santa. Be sure and have parents go with you to help out watching the children. Also, ask ahead of time if you could take a group picture with Santa Claus. If a mall isn't near to you, look for areas nearby that have been decorated and go there instead. Some areas have elk or "reindeer" farms you can visit.

An alternate activity to visiting with Santa at a mall, is make arrangements for someone to wear a rented Santa suit and talk with each child at school and give them each a small toy that you have purchased ahead of time or a bag with an orange and peanuts in it. Get a picture with each child sitting on Santa's lap with a digital camera. Then develop/print them and give them to the children in a frame.

Machines and Tools

GROUP ACTIVITIES/CIRCLE TIME

MUSIC AND MOVEMENT

"Bumping Up and Down" from Singable Songs for the Very Young" CD & tape by Raffi.

"Working on the Railroad" from "Singable Collection- Part 2" CD & tape by Raffi. Children enjoy singing along with this old familiar song.

"The Number Rock" from "We All Live Together Vol. 2" CD & tape by Greg Scelsa.

"Dancin' Machine" from "We All Live Together Vol. 3" CD & tape by Greg Scelsa. Children have fun dancing and moving like a washing machine, egg beater, oil well, train, robot, and an airplane.

"Mashed Potatoes" from "Jim Gill Sings Do Re Mi on His Toe Leg Knee" CD by Jim Gill.

"I Took a Bath in a Washing Machine" from "Jim Gill Sings The Sneezing Song and other Contagious Tunes" CD by Jim Gill.

"Jimmy Jones Built A Car" by Jean Warren from More Piggyback Songs, Totline Press. In this song, children sing to a turn they already know - "Old MacDonald Had a Farm." Like the original song, the children participate also by saying their name, what they are building, and naming the tool that they are using.

"The Robot Song" by Serena K. Butch from More Piggyback Songs, Totline Press. This song is sung to the tune "Wheels on the Bus." Children move as a robot - arms up and down, legs back and forth, head side to side, etc. This is a fun movement song that is easy to learn.

"My Favorite Machine" by Lynn Beaird, from Piggyback Songs, Totline Press. This is to the tune of "My Bonnie Lies Over the Ocean." This song lets you and the children learn about various machines and how they work.

"Johnny's Hammers" is sung to the tune of "Mary Had a Little Lamb." This is a fun song for children to move to. They use their hands, feet, and head as hammers in this song.

Johnny's Hammers

Johnny had 1 hammer, 1 hammer, 1 hammer (Make hammering motion with a single fist)

Johnny had 1 hammer, then he had 2.

Johnny had 2 hammers, 2 hammers, 2 hammers, (Make hammering motion with both fists)

Johnny had 2 hammers, then he had 3.

Johnny had 3 hammers, 3 hammers, 3 hammers, (Make motion with both fists and one leg)

Johnny had 3 hammers then he had 4.

Johnny had 4 hammers, 4 hammers, 4 hammers, (Make motion with both fists and both legs)

Johnny had 4 hammers then he had 5.

Johnny had 5 hammers, 5 hammers, 5 hammers (Make motion with both fists, both legs and head)

Johnny had 5 hammers, then he went to sleep! (put hands like sleeping)

"The Robot in the House" by Sharlit Elliot is sung to the tune of "The Farmer in the Dell."

The Robot in the House

The robot in the house,

The robot in the house,

Hi! Ho! The der-ry oh,

The robot in the house.

The robot uses the vacuum,

The robot uses the vacuum,

Hi! Ho! The der-ry oh,

The robot in the house.

(continue verses)

3. The robot uses the blender . . .

4. The robot uses the toaster . . .

5. The robot uses the hammer . . .

6. The robot uses the drill . . .

7. The robot uses the iron . . .

8. The robot uses the washer . . .

9. The robot uses the dryer . . .

Children sing the song in the same manner as in verses one and two. Children can sing the verses in any order and they can add other machines used in the house. You can use pictures of machines with the song. Another day, you could change the song to – "The children in the class . . ."

Then sing – "The children use the _____." Let them list the things that they use in their class.

LANGUAGE AND LITERACY

Bam Bam Bam by Bill Martin, Scholastic, Inc.

Mike Mulligan and His Steam Shovel by Virginia Lee Burton, Scholastic, Inc.

The Home Depot Big Book of Tools by Kimberly Weinberger, Scholastic, Inc.

I've Been Working on the Railroad by Nadine Westcott, Trumpet an associated logo of Scholastic, Inc.

If I Had A Robot by Dan Yaccarino, Scholastic, Inc.

The Garden in Our Yard by Greg Henry Quinn, Scholastic, Inc. This book show boys and girls using garden tools to plant and grow things.

What's Inside? Toys by Dorling Kindersley Book, Dorling Kindersley, New York.

Robots Slither by Ryan Ann Hunter, G.P. Putnum's Sons, New York.

The Toolbox by Ann Rockwell, Macmillan, New York.

Everyday Machines and How They Work by Herman Schneider, McGraw-Hill.

Tool Book by Gail Gibbons, Holiday House, New York.

Tools and Gadgets by Bobbie Kalman, Crabtree, New York 1992.

Tools by Ann Morris Lothrop, Lee & Shepard 1999.

Robots Kids Discover, Kids Discover Series.

Robots! by Peter Borough, N.H. Cobblestones.

Robots Among Us: The Challenges and Promise of Robotics by Christopher Baker Millbrook, Brookfield & Company.

Kitchen Science Experiments by QL Pearce, Contemporary, Chicago.

Science Around Us Using Machines by Sally Hewitt, Chrysalis Education.

Machines At Work by Byron Baxton, Harper Collins.

Robots by Clive Gifford, North Mankato, Smart Apple Medic, 2006

LANGUAGE AND LITERACY ACTIVITIES

Introduce to the children what a tool does. Explain to them that a tool helps us do work. In advance, buy two packages of instant pudding of the same flavor. Have the children wash their hands before coming to the circle or before starting the activity. Tell them that they will be making pudding and they need clean hands.

Have the following items ready: two boxes of pudding, two bowls to mix it in, milk, spoon to mix, a hand egg beater or hand held mixer. Have the children help you empty the pudding into the bowls and add the correct amount of milk in each bowl.

Now, have children take turns mixing the two bowls. In one bowl, use a spoon to mix the pudding. In the other bowl, use hand or electric mixer. Time how long it takes each tool to mix the pudding. Give the children the times of how long each took to get the job done. Ask which tool did the fastest job. Tell them that power tools can help us work faster and save time. At the end of the activity, have small cups and spoons to give each child a taste of the pudding.

On the second day of the unit, bring different kitchen tools and machines to class such as a can opener, toaster, potato peeler, grater, blender, and timer. Show each tool and ask children how the tool works. Then demonstrate their use.

On the third day, bring garden tools such as a rake, shovel, hoe, watering can, a sprayer, pruners and grass cutters. Discuss with the children how and why these tools are used. Also explain how to be safe while using tools. Later, take the children outside to play and bring out potatoes, carrots, and green onions for the children to pretend to plant in the sand box. Also, take out some of the tools like the shovel and the rake for children to use.

On the fourth day, bring in a tool box with screwdrivers, a hammer, level, power drill, saw, pliers, wrench and tape measure. Take the tools out one at a time and ask children what they think it is and how it is used. Then demonstrate how it is used. Use the drill to make small holes in wood. Then provide wood screws for the children screw into the wood holes using the screw driver. Also put out on a table some hammers with nails and boards. Talk about safety before they leave the circle and give them a rule to put goggles on before using a hammer.

You can also read books on robots such as Robots! by Peter Borough and talk about real robots that are used in assembly lines or with hazardous things. Show pictures of some of them. Ask children if they have any questions. You can also add clips from shows such as "How It's Made" which shows different types of products being produced.

Have several boxes large boxes with arm holes cut in them and have them covered with foil. Ask children to help you glue buttons and other misc items to make them into robots. Ask children how they think a robot might walk. Then let the children try on the box robot and walk around the circle. Then let other children take turns wearing one.

Another day, talk about computers and printers with the children. Ask what they know about them and if they have one at home. Also ask questions such as: "What we do with computers?" and "How do they help us?" If you have one in your room, show them some of the things that they can do besides play games.

SMALL GROUP ACTIVITIES/TABLE TIMES

MATH & COGNITIVE

Shape Machine Matches

You will use mini sized construction toys or die cuts of machines for this activity. Tape or glue various shapes on the toys or die cuts, having two of each shape per set. Then have the children match the shapes in their set and name the shapes.

Another way to play this game is to use several sets together. Place them in the center of the table and children will take turns choosing two that are the same and naming them. Then the next player in the circle will take a turn. Play will continue until all of the machines are matched up.

Sorting Screws

Ask parents ahead of time to have the children bring in odd screws, nuts, bolts, etc., they have around their home that are not needed. After they have been collected, provide a sorting tray for the children to sort the materials into groups that are similar in different ways. You can use muffin tins to sort in or even things like empty small boxes.

After the children have sorted them, talk with the children think that they are the same and/or different from each other. Then with your help they can count them and learn which group has the most and which group has the least.

Measuring Game

Show the children a measuring tape and demonstrate how it works. Tell the children that they will make their own special measure to measure with.

Trace around each child's hand or their foot. Then cover the foot or hand with clear contact paper and cut them. Be sure they have their names written on them. Have each child use his/her special measure to measure items in the room such as the table or chairs. They will place their special hand or foot on the object to be measured and count how many of them it takes to go from top to bottom or across from left to right.

After they have done this for a day, have them estimate (guess) how many hands or feet long an object will be. Then write each child's estimate down with their name and then measure it to see how close they came.

House Building

Have a few of the children come to the table at a time. Have various tools such as screw drivers, pliers and hammers at the table. Ask the children to tell which screwdriver is long and which is short. Also, ask which tools are big and small.

Provide small building blocks or Legos that fit on tables. The children will be directed to build one big house and one small house.

Counting Activity

Obtain some soft boards from a lumber yard. Some of the yards will give you scrap pieces for no charge. Also, buy small nails with large heads. Borrow or buy a few hammers.

For this activity, children will pound nails into the boards and then count how many nails they put into their board. Next, they will use a number line to find the number that they have and tell others how many and which numeral represents that amount. You can buy number lines at a school supply store or make your own. Have children put their names on the board and have them take their great accomplishment home.

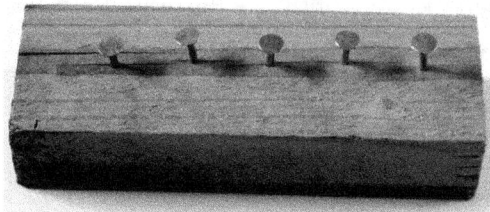

Tool Headband

Buy stickers of tools at a scrapbook store or a school supply store. If not available, make copies of tools that you draw or shrink and copy ones from advertisements or catalogs. Make a master copy of the patterns on a piece of copy paper with even spaces on page, so they can be copied and cut apart with a paper cutter when completed. Children will be making a pattern using the tool pictures. They will be gluing the pictures in a pattern on long strips of white paper. If this is their first time of making a pattern, they should lay pictures out in the order of a two tool pattern. Teacher will check to be sure it was done correctly and then children will glue them onto their strip of paper. If they want to wear it right away, use glue sticks because they quick drying, while regular glue will take time to dry before the bands can be worn.

Robot Shape Match

Make small tube robots for children to use at table or use the "robot" they made in fine motor activity. Use a plastic shape or make paper ones. Place the shapes in the middle of the table.

Then children will take turns having their robot find the shape that the teacher names.

Children will use the robot to touch the correct shape and then say the shape's name. If they found the correct shape, they will keep that shape on the table by them. When all of the shapes have been named correctly, they will count the shapes that they each have. There is no single winner, all the children are winners. The directions to make robot is in this unit under fine motor skills.

FINE MOTOR SKILLS

Robot

Provide various paper towel rolls, tubes from waxed paper, small boxes from pudding and etc. Children will use foil to cover their tub or box to create their own robot .The teacher will help them tear off a piece of foil long enough to cover their container. Children will cover the tube with the foil and use permanent markers to draw on the details of their robot. They can use small buttons, wiggle plastic eyes or paper hole reinforcement to make eyes and sparkly pipe cleaners to create antennas. Be sure and have glue available for them to use.

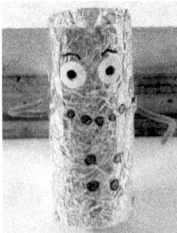

Tools and Toolbox

Draw simple tool shapes like a hammer, saw and screw driver. See example. Then make copies for each child.

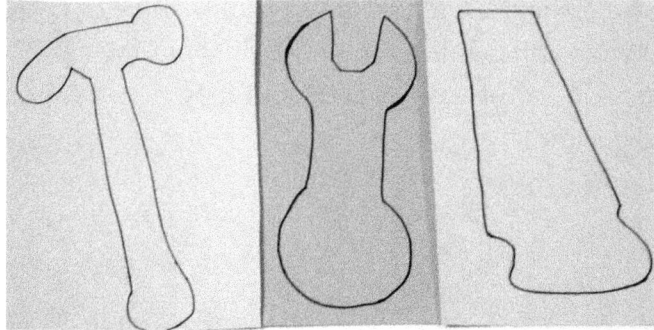

On the first day, the children will fold a piece of colored construction paper over and staple the sides together to make a toolbox. Next, they will cut out one of the tools that you have talked about that day. They will place it in their tool box when it has been cut out. During the remainder of the week, children will cut out the rest of the tools as you talk about them. When it is complete, have the children take them home. They can tell their parents all about the tools in their tool box.

Tool Painting

Purchase kitchen tools such as a potato mashers, egg circle whips, and any other tools that will leave interesting prints. Use foam bakery trays to place different colors of paint. Give each child a long piece of white paper and let them make prints using the ends of the tools. They will dip into the paint and then place end of tool on the paper to create a print. See example.

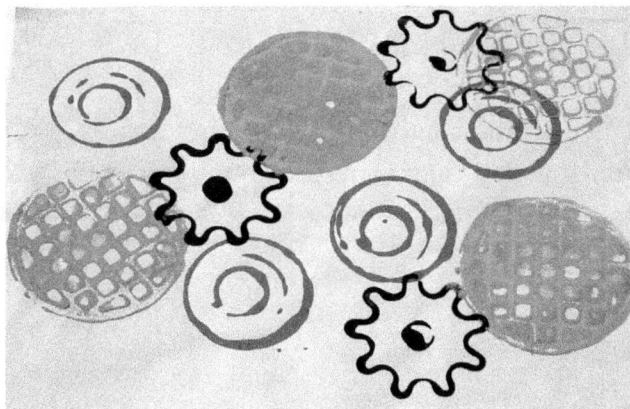

Tool Puzzle

Use plastic toy tools or larger real tools for this activity. Teacher will place the tools one at a time on poster board and trace around each tool's shape. Laminate the pictures. The children will take turns placing the correct tool shape on the matching shape. You can also have them name the shape. The tool must match and not be turned the incorrect way. This can be tricky for some children because they put the correct tool on the shape, but it won't match unless it is turned correctly and they may even have to flip it over to match the shapes. See example.

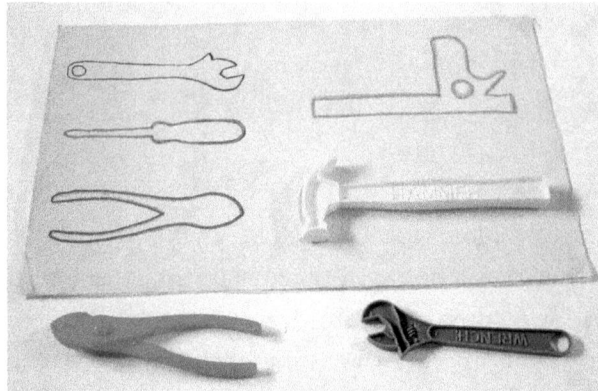

Computer

Print out a copy of the letters and numbers on your keyboard for each child. They will glue this to the bottom half of a piece of the long colored construction paper.

Make several a tracer patterns for a computer screen. Give out the tracers and have children trace and cut out a screen for their computer and glue it on the top part of the long construction paper above the keyboard so that it resembles a real computer.

Now the children will use markers or crayons to draw a picture of what they would like to have on their computer screen. It could be a computer game, an E-mail letter to someone or a picture of whatever they want. Use this on the day that you talk about computers. See example.

Bolts and Boards

Prepare boards with holes drilled into them and fitted with bolts with nuts to match correct size of hole. Children will fit the bolt into the holes on their board and screw the nut on the end of the bolt.

Supply soft wood and wood screws with screw drivers. Children will screw the short screws into the boards.

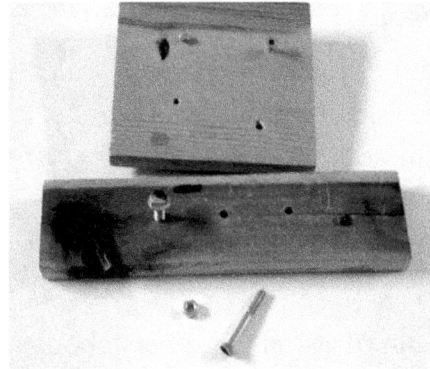

Machine

Have craft sticks, milk bottle lids, small pieces of Styrofoam, metal frozen juice lids, cut egg cartons and anything else you can think of for the children to glue together to make their own machine. Provide a paper plate for them to make their machine on, so that it can be moved off the table to dry out of the way,

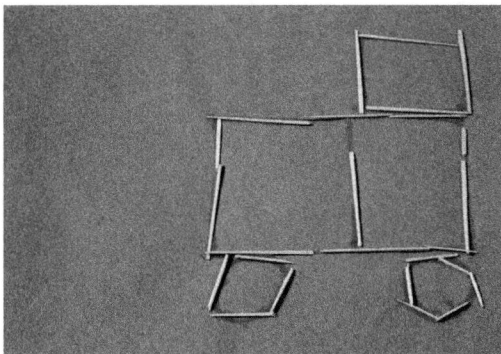

Collage

Provide the children with markers, glue, paper, scissors, craft sticks, colored toothpicks, pipe cleaners, paper clips and construction paper. Tell the children to make a picture of some type of a machine with the materials provided.

LANGUAGE AND LITERACY

Name That Sound

Use a recorder to tape various sounds that machines make such as a toilet flushing, a lawnmower running, a toaster popping up, a mixer going, a person hammering, a fan blowing, a phone ringing, a saw sawing, scissors cutting and a car or truck running.

Tell the children listen carefully to the tape and raise their hands when they can identify the sounds they heard. Have a short discussion of the sounds after hearing them. Ask how they knew it has a (saw, name the sound) Have they heard that sound before? How was it being used?

Name That Tool

Get out materials such as ruler, potato peeler, can opener, screw drivers – both Phillips and flathead, level, alarm clock, air pump, hole punch, kitchen whip, tongs, and nail clippers. Children will take turns identifying a tool and telling how you use it.

Drawing

Have the children draw their own tool with paper and markers. Then have the children take turns telling others about what the tool does to help us. Write the children words on a paper and attach it to his/her drawing.

Put them all together to make a book by punching holes and in them and binding with yarn or inside a folder. Then later that day or the next day, get their book out and reading it do everyone. Be sure and write who made each page. Then place it out so they can read and look at it when they want.

Naming Positions

Acquire small shoe boxes or use other small boxes for a toolbox. Buy plastic tools in a toy store or a Dollar type store. Let each child at the table choose a tool and a box to place it in. Teacher will give directions to tell children where to move their tool. Example under their box, over their box, in front of their box, behind their box, in their box, out of their box and etc.

Children will follow the teacher's directions. Only use a few directions over and over until they understand where to put it. You can also do it with them, so that they can see where it goes. Later on, when they know the placements better, have them take turns telling the others where to put their tool.

Kitchen Tools

Provide different sizes of kitchen tools, such as a large wooden spoons, medium spoons and small spoons. The children will be asked to put the spoons in order from largest to smallest. Use words with them as directions such as "show me the bigger one," "place the next bigger one there" and so on. Next have them tell you using their words, not by pointing how to arrange the tools.

Sorting Tools

Provide different types of tools such as kitchen tools, garden hand tools and woodworking tools. Children will take turns naming each tool. Then talk about how the different tools are used. Ask if they can see a tool that is like another one in some way. Keep asking questions until the children are able to group the tools that go together in different categories.

What's Missing?

Place four tools on the table. They can be any type that the children are learning about. All together, say each tool's name. Then cover them up with a towel and have the children close their eyes. Remove one of them. Don't let the children see which one you took away. Now have them open their eyes and raise their hand or take turns calling on them to tell you which item is missing. Play continues with the same tools until they know all the names and then introduce a new one.

FREE TIME

CREATIVE ARTS

Play Dough

Children will use play dough to model tools and or machines. Provide several different colors for them to work with. Also, have craft sticks to put the clay around to add strength to their designs.

<u>Soft Play Dough</u>

2 cups flour	2 Tbs. cream of tartar
1 cup salt	2 Tbs. cooking oil
2 cups water	*food coloring optional

Combine all ingredients in a medium sauce pan. Mix well. Cook over low heat stirring constantly until mixture gathers and forms a dough. Dump onto counter until cool enough to handle and then knead to form a ball. Store in a container or plastic bag.

*Food coloring may be added to the water before. Mixing with the flour.

Finger Painting

Put finger paint paper out for children to use for this activity. Tell the children to create any design they would like. When the pictures are dry, hang them up around the room. Make sure that there are many bright colors for them to use. Children should have aprons on for this activity. Hint - it's less messy to have a pail with warm soapy water on the counter for them to wash most of the paint off their hands versus when they turn on the tap in the bathroom, where it is easy to get paint everywhere.

SENSORY

Place sand in large pails or in a sensory tub with mini construction toys, like cement trucks. Also include small blocks for buildings and craft sticks for fences. Small toy people are also great to place in the pails. You can find these things in toy departments and some school supply stores.

You can also use water in the sensory table with scoops and water wheels. Children love to see the wheels go around when they pour the water to make it go. Water wheels are easier to find in the summer months for sand box uses, but they can be used all year long.

DRAMATIC PLAY & SOCIAL DEVELOPMENT

Set out child sized construction hard hats for children to wear along with tools and work aprons. You can make child sized aprons. The Home Depot has these aprons and has given them to the children in my class when they have gone on a field trip there. The tools can be real or toys. The children can pretend to be builders using wood blocks to build things.

Another idea is for the children to be a sales clerk in a hardware store. Have carpenter aprons, cash registers, wood blocks, sacks, nails, screws and tools to use with their hardware store or a fix it shop.

Children can make a sign for their store with a little help. Play money can be made by cutting green construction paper into small rectangles and adding a dollar sign with a number. Also have chipboards with paper and pencils to write down their orders.

SCIENCE

Place a broken machine of some type such as an old alarm clock, radio etc. on the table. It is best if it has screws that can be undone. Make sure that the cord is cut off from electrical thing that children will be using. That will help them not get hurt while trying to take it apart.

Even better is to have more than one thing to take apart and discover how it's put together. Ask parents to donate items that no longer work or go to an as is store to obtain items. Make sure you provide screw drivers and even pliers in many sizes and different types.

Place books on the table that show pictures of different types of machines that you think your children will be interested in.

GROSS MOTOR SKILLS

Use the song "I Took A Bath In A Washing Machine" by Jim Gill found under Music and Movement. The children have fun acting out what it would be like in the washing machine.

Another great song to have children act out is "Dancing Machine" by Greg Scelsa also in the Music and Movement section in the front of the unit.

For this movement activity, have the children take turns showing the class a movement that they can do such as touching their toes. Then the class will do the same movement together. Next another child will do a different movement that the class will copy. This activity continues until children are starting to lose interest. Keep track of those that have had a turn so when you do this activity again you'll know who still needs a turn another day. Make sure the children see this list and know that their turn is still coming.

One more fun activity is the "Silly Dance Contest" found on the CD <u>Jim Gill Sings The Sneezing Song and other Contagious Tunes</u> by Jim Gill. This simple song gets everyone moving.

FIELD TRIP IDEAS

Arrange a field trip to a hardware store such as Home Depot or Lowes. Tell them that you would like them to show you the tools and how they are used. They usually will have the children make something while there or plant something. There are lots of things to see. It would be good to talk about what the children would like to see before going and what questions they have so that the field trip will cover these areas.

Also, have the children make pictures for them. Place their pictures inside a cover. The cover could have children's stamped hand prints on it in various poster paint colors. Be sure and include the name of your school on the cover with the words "Thank You" written on it.

Take your camera and take lots of pictures of the children and any parents that went with you for the children's scrap books.

Fairy Tales in Three's

This unit covers "The Three Bears," "The Three Little Pigs," "The Three Little Kittens," and "The Three Billy Goats Gruff."

GROUP ACTIVITIES/CIRCLE TIME

MUSIC AND MOVEMENT

"The Cool Bear Hunt" from "Dr. Jean Sings Silly Songs" CD.

"Bringing Home A Baby Bumble Bee" from "Dr. Jean Sings Silly Songs" CD.

"Bear Went Over The Mountain" from "Dr. Jean Sings Silly Songs" CD.

"The Three Boppin Bear Rap" from "Dr. Jean Sings Silly Songs" CD.

"Grandmother's Farm" from "Witches' Brew" by Hap Palmer.

"Across The Bridge" from "We All Live Together" Vol. 3 by Greg Scelsa. Children do these movements while going over a balance beam or tape line for the bridge: walk across the bridge, walk sideways... left foot first, walk sideways ...right foot first, last take giant steps.

"Dance Medley" from "We All Live Together" Vol. 3 by Greg Scelsa. This is a fun song that directs the children to do school house twist, walk like an elephant, swim, stroll, do the duck walk and glide like a snake.

"Safe and Calm" from "Brain Boogie Boosters" by The Learning Station & Dr. Becky Bailey CD.

"Brain Game" Brain Boogie Boosters" by The Learning Station & Dr. Becky Bailey CD.

Teachers, pick and choose from these different types of songs. Create a balance of active and calm songs. It's also very important to not sing all new songs that the children don't know, so be sure and include their old favorites too.

LANGUAGE AND LITERACY

The Three Billy Goats Gruff with pictures by Stephen Carpenter, Scholastic Inc.

Three Little Kittens with pictures by Lilian Obligado, A Random House Pictureback.

The Three Bears retold by Dandi, Landoll, Inc.

The Silly Story of Goldie Locks and the Three Squares by Grace Maccarone, Scholastic Inc. This book is a fun way to teach about math after the children have become familiar with the original story of The Three Bears.

Beware of the Bears! by Alan MacDonald, Scholastic Inc. This book is a fun take off on what the three bears tried to do to Goldilocks after she messes up their house.

The Three Little Pigs Modern Publishing, A Division of Unisystems, Inc. This story is the traditional one.

The Three Little Pigs retold and illustrated by Gavin Bishop, Scholastic Inc.

The Three Little Pigs retold and illustrated by James Marshall, Scholastic Inc.

The Three Little Wolves and the Big Bad Pig by Eugene Trivizas, Scholastic Inc. This story is a reversal similar to The Three Little Pigs. It's a fun way to see that like all characters in books are not the same just because they are the same animal, just as in life not all people are the same. People are all different no matter what nationality or color of their skin.

Teachers, read the traditional stories many times. The children love them and the repetition helps them to learn. Also, have them join in with you as you read to them by saying the repeated words with you. An example would be the phrase, "I'll Huff and Puff and I'll Blow Your House In."

When the children have the story lines well learned use bought flannel story figures such as the one manufactured by The Story Teller which has an online store now at http://www.funfelt.com/products.html.

You can also make your own figures using clip art or coloring book pictures. Laminate your pictures and add sticky magnet pieces to their backs. Then let the children use the figures to retell the story to others or to you.

SMALL GROUP ACTIVITIES/TABLE TIMES

MATH & COGNITIVE

Piggy Bank Cards

Draw a simple pig pattern on colored construction paper. Then make copies of the pig by placing the pig over multiple sheets of pink paper and cutting out the top copy pattern through all the sheets. Make five to ten copies. Then write a different number on each of the pigs with a marker and laminate them. Bring a bag of pennies, enough for the amount of numbers on the pigs.

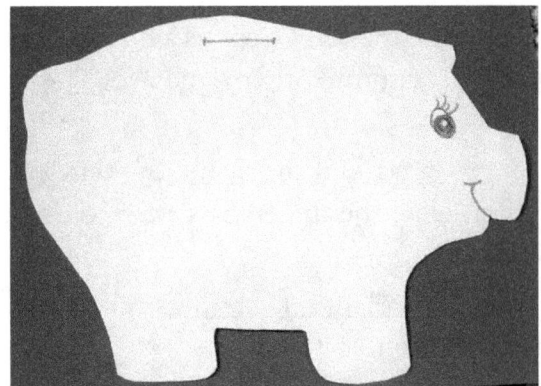

Children will say the numeral name with you and count that many pennies to go on the piggy bank. Play continues until all members of the group have had a turn with the different pigs saying and counting the numbers.

Bear Cards

Punch out bears using a die or copy them from clip art. You will need a set of ten for each person to use at the table. Write on the front of the bear the numbers one through ten on each set. Then using a marker or tiny dot stickers, place that amount on the back of the bear that matches the number that is on the front of each card. Next laminate all the cards.

If the children are just learning their numbers start out with the bears numbered one to three. Have the children say the numeral names and then put the number bears in order 1-3. If they don't recognize the number, have them turn them over and count the dots on the back.

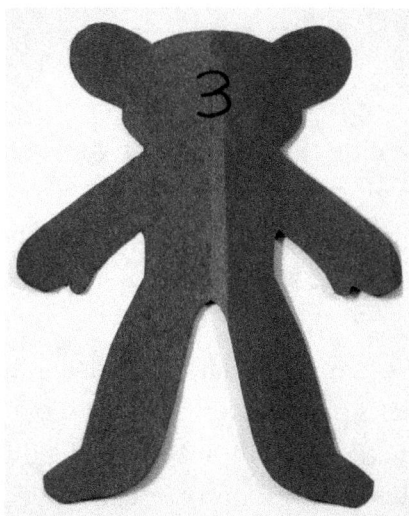

Over a period of time, the children will learn their numbers. As the children learn the numbers, increase the numbers on the bears until they can say the numbers 1-10 and put them in correct order. See example.

Block Patterns

Put out small square blocks for the children to make block patterns. Show a simple six block pattern to the children. Don't show how to make it, but will tell them to make it look just like yours. See example.

If they can't get it after trying a couple of times, show them how to do it. Have them do it with your help. Then tell them to make a bridge for the goats. Provide plastic small goats.

Kitten Shapes

Cut out a large kitten head and place lines on it like a bingo type card. Make a card for each of the children in your small group to use. See example.

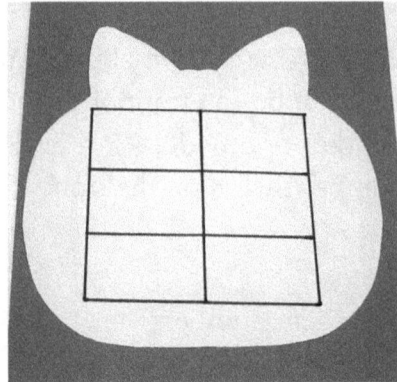

Decide the shapes that you want the children to learn such as a triangle, square, circle, oval, diamond, rectangle, etc. Place a different shape in each square on the kitten head. The shapes can be drawn on the card or cut from colored construction paper and glued onto the squares. Then laminate them.

Next, make a large die using an empty milk carton that has been cut flat and covered with plain paper or buy a large foam die and cut six pieces of square paper to glue over each of the sides. Now add a different shape to each side of the die. Use the same shapes that you put on your cards. Use beans or buttons to cover the shapes during play.

The game is played by taking turns rolling the die. Children identify the die that is facing up and cover the die on their card that matches it. If the players shake a shape that they have already covered they may shake one more time. If the player still doesn't get the needed shape they can cover their shape when someone else rolls the shape that they need. Play continues with the next person rolling the die and identifying it and covering the matching shape on their card. This continues until all of the shapes have been covered.

Pattern Bridge

Cut out two or more different colors of squares. Provide construction paper and glue. Children will make a long bridge across their paper using two or three colored squares forming a pattern that repeats itself across the sheet. First, have the children show you their pattern before gluing it down. Talk about how a pattern repeats and then have them start to glue their pattern down. Check to make sure that they still understand how to make a pattern and have them continue with their pattern across the sheet.

FINE MOTOR SKILLS

Finger Paint

Children will draw pigs on paper and then cut around them. These pigs will be used to put in their pretend mud. Children will use chocolate pudding to finger paint pretend mud on a piece of card stock or other heavy weight paper. Then have the child place their cut out pigs on their mud.

Billy Goat Bridge

Make salt dough and color it any color that you would like. Children will create a bridge by flattening pieces of play dough and/or rolling pieces into long ropes in the manner that they want it. Children will model the dough on a paper plate or something sturdy so that it can be moved and left to dry.

<u>Self Hardening Play Dough</u>

4 cups flour	1 Tsp. alum
11/2 cups salt	* Optional 1 - 2 Tbs. food coloring

Mix the flour, salt and alum together. Then add the water to it gradually. *If you want mixture colored, add coloring to water before stirring into the flour for a smooth color. Stir to form a ball in bowl. Add more water if it won't hold together, Next knead dough. Place in a sealed container until ready to use. After shapes have been made leave out to dry.

You can place the bridges on a cookie sheet covered with foil and bake them at a low temperature (about 100° F) to speed up the drying time. When it has dried, children can take it home or they can use markers or paint to decorate it before taking it home. The bridge can also be placed on a paper plate with a pretend blue river under it.

Puzzles

Go to any school supply or regular store where you can purchase puzzles with fairy tale figures on them. Set the puzzles out and have the children figure out how to put them together. Sit close by so that they can see you doing a puzzle. As you put them together mention advice that will help them, such as "I'm finding the bears head" or "These colors are the same, they must go together."

Make Your Own Puzzles

Many school districts have dye cuts that will allow you to punch out puzzle pieces. If your area does, you could ask them to let you cut one for each of your children. Another place to purchase blank, small, and square puzzles is through school supply stores or you can also buy them through school supply catalogues and have items mailed to you.

You can also cut small squares on white poster board and have the children make their drawings on them. Once you have the blank puzzle squares or poster board squares, children can draw their own pictures to represent fairy tale figures on them.

If you use the poster boards then you will have the children draw lines on the backs where they could be cut out. Make sure you have them draw only three or four pieces so that the puzzle isn't too difficult. Then they can cut them out on the lines.

Have the children put either type of puzzle together and then place the pieces in a small zip lock bag to keep the pieces together. Write their name on the bag and the name of the puzzle they made. (Example: The Three Bears) Keep these in the class in a shoe box so that children can use all the puzzles. They can take their own puzzle home when the challenge of doing them is no longer there.

Kitten Mitten

Cut out a large mitten pattern. Then make five or six tracings of that pattern on poster board and cut them out. Children will use a pencil to trace the outside of the mitten pattern onto long watercolor paper. Children can then cut out the pattern or if you prefer, just use the lines of the mitten without cutting it out. Next, the children will use watercolors to decorate and draw anything that they would like. When the paintings are dry hang them up on a rope using clothes pins. Add a label saying "These are the kitten's lost mittens." See example.

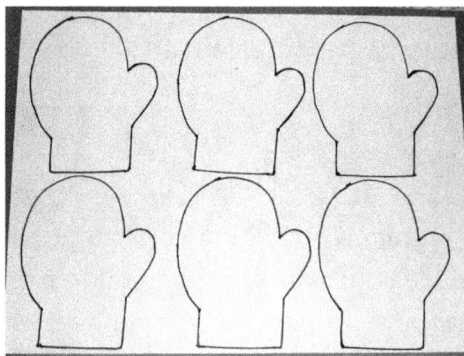

LANGUAGE AND LITERACY

Pig Order

Prepare a set of four pigs in various sizes. Use clip art online or coloring books to find a pictures of a pig or draw one. Then make various sizes of the pigs by using a copy machine or blowing them up on your computer. Make as many sets as you will need to work with a few children at a small table.

Have the children tell you verbally and place in order pigs from largest to smallest. Say which one is the largest, the next largest and so on until they have named and put in order the pigs from largest to smallest. Then when they are in order, have them label their sizes by saying the sizes to you while pointing to them.

Next time, have the children start with the smallest pig and go up until reaching the largest small pig. Then proceed as before by saying and pointing to the pigs in proper sequence.

Name That Item

Collect items that were talked about in one of the fairytale stories such as the story of The Three Bears. These items could be a pan, bowl, spoon, small pillow, a small blanket, or a teddy bear.

Place the items in a large black plastic bag. Children will take turns putting their hand into the bag without looking and try to identify one of the items from the story by feeling it. They will make a guess and then pull the item out. Next, they will tell what the item is and how it was used in the story. For example - the bowl held the porridge or cereal. Ask another child how the cereal or porridge was different from the other ones. (Hot, cold and just right). Continue in this manner until all the items in the bag have been talked about.

This activity will help the children to recall, increase their vocabulary and help them to use more expressive language.

Three Little Pigs

After reading The Three Little Pigs, talk to the children about emotions. Tell them that emotions means how you or someone else feels. Ask them how they would feel if they didn't have a place to live. Do you think that the pigs felt the same way? How would you feel if someone gave you the things that you needed to make a home? What did each of the pigs receive to build their home? How did they feel when the wolf knocked on their do and wanted to come inside? How did the wolf feel when he was chasing the pigs? Do you sometimes feel angry? What is it like to be mad?

Have them use their voice and body to show how they look and act when they are mad. Keep asking questions that relate to the story and explore different emotions. Be sure and end on a happy and positive note. The pigs felt happy when the wolf went away. Tell us what makes you feel happy?

Your Story of the Three Kittens

After reading the story of The Three Little Kittens have your children draw what they think the three kittens might do next. Use markers or crayons with white paper. Next, have each of the children tell you what is happening in their picture and write their words of their paper.

When all the pictures and words have been completed read all the papers by the different children. You could also put all the papers in a three ring binder, so the children could read their stories and the other children's stories whenever they wanted.

The Three Billy Goats Gruff

Make cards using card stock or index cards. Glue goat pictures on the front sides of them. You can use goat stickers or clip art from books or online. On the back of each card write a different statement for the children to do.

Have the children pick a card and you will read it to them. The card will say various things for them to say and do. Then ask them to do it.

Examples:

- Act like you're a small goat that has lost its family and tell us what you would say and do to get others to help you get back home.

- Show us how you would act if you were the middle size goat and you were afraid of going over a bridge by yourself.

- Tell what you would do and say if you were the troll and others wanted to cross your bridge.

One of the cards could also say pretend that you have magic horns on your head and that you can grant wishes to others. Have them pick another child and ask them what they would wish for if you could grant them their wishes. Then tell the child why you would or wouldn't grant their wish. When they have had a turn they will choose someone else to be the magic goat.

FREE TIME

CREATIVE ARTS

Cut out a large pig shape like in the example "Piggy Bank Cards" for each child. Then set out a large lid from a box with sides on it about three inches high around it. You can purchase boxes at an office supply store that have lids like that or you can use another box that doesn't have a lid and cut the sides down on it. The sides on the lid help to keep things inside it.

Children will be rolling golf balls inside the box over various colors of poster paint. Children will first write their name on the pig cutout and place their name side down in the box lid, so that the paint will not cover their name up. Let them choose the colors that they would like on their pig and have them put small spoonfuls of paint on their pig.

Next children will carefully tilt the box from side to side to roll the balls onto the pig pattern. When they are finished, hang them up to dry and enjoy their colorful pictures posted in your room.

Once they have learned how to do this project, on another day draw and cut out other pattern shapes and roll the balls in different colors on them.

Another fun project for this week is to have the children watercolor pictures of the fairy tales that you have talked about and create a picture book. They could also add words to their pictures when they are dry by telling a teacher what is happening in their picture.

SENSORY

Buy moon sand from a school supply store or from a toy store. Place the sand in pails or a sensory table with toy molds or other simple things you already have such as cups and cartons. Children place the sand inside of the objects and push them down tight and then turn them over quickly to release the sand. The sand will hold the shape of the container. You can use small cake or gelatin molds for this also.

Another fun thing to put into the pails or sensory table is flour with flour shifters, different shapes of small baking pans and small bowls with spoons for stirring. They can also mold with flour but it is harder for them to turn it over to release it without it falling apart.

DRAMATIC PLAY & SOCIAL DEVELOPMENT

Place different props that match the fairytale you are talking about for the children to play with. The children will use these props to act out the stories you do in your class. For example, on the days you talk about The Three Pigs, place head bands made of elastic with felt triangle ears sewn on the band to represent the pigs in the story. Then add wolf ears by using large brown pieces on a head band.

Place blocks out for them to build houses. The large paper blocks work the best because they can then build them large enough to get inside their "houses." Also, if they fall on the children, they won't hurt them.

Provide poster board with markers for them to draw other type of houses such as wood or straw. They then can place them in front of their block houses to change them. If you have lots of blocks and it's warm, they could build them outside and tape the poster drawings on the front of their houses.

Children really enjoy acting out the story, especially running in and out of the houses while the wolf chases them.

Another idea would be to act out <u>Three Billy Goats Gruff</u> story. Make head bands for the three different sized goats using poster board ears on a strips of white paper to form a head band. The size of the ears will be small, medium and large. Then buy a simple headband with floppy things that stick up for the troll. You can usually get these at a Dollar store. You can also make simple beards in different sizes to represent the different sized goats using poster paper and applying it with rolled masking tape to their chins. Also, make signs to hang around children's neck that say who they are such as "small billy goat gruff" or "troll." See example.

To make a bridge you can use two chairs placed apart with a sheet over them to look, where the troll can hide. Another thing that works for a bridge is a wood boat rocker that when turned upside down becomes steps that go up and down. This wood rocker is found in school catalogs under classroom furniture. It makes a great bridge for the children to use when acting out the story.

Now explain the props to the children and have them take turns with them while they enjoy acting out the story.

SCIENCE

Put a balancing scale out for the science table. You can buy this at school supply store. You will also need small plastic animals. A farm animal set works best. There are four different colors of each animal. Children will place different amounts of the animals in the cups on each side of the scale to see it they can make them balance. They will enjoy spending time there experimenting with the animals in the scale cups.

Ask them questions while they are trying out different amounts such as, what might happen if you put two more pigs on the right side of the scale. Then have them tell you what happened. Ask other questions to get them thinking and figuring out how to balance.

If you can't purchase farm animals, you could use small toys from the birthday party favor section of a store such as the dollar store. You could also so use small rocks or sea shells for balancing.

GROSS MOTOR SKILLS

If possible, have the children go outside for this activity and have them gallop like goats. Children learn to gallop before they can skip. They could next walk around growling like a bear or running like a wolf.

If you are doing this activity inside, ask them to be different animals. They could act like a dog, being down on all fours crawling, a rabbit could hop, and a snake could slither while lying on the floor. They can help name different animals and move their body as they think the animals would move.

FIELD TRIP IDEAS

Arrange to have the children visit an animal shelter or a farm. If at a farm, learn the different animal names and what the animals do at the farm. Find out what they eat and how they live.

If at an animal shelter, have the workers explain how the animals got there. Have the children also find out what they can do to help keep animals safe and how to care properly for animals.

Be sure and bring a thank you card made by the children to take with you for them. This could be their drawings of animals or anything that they wanted to draw. Also, have parents go with you to help with the children and take lots of pictures of the children with the animals.

Where To Get What You Need

There are many different places to get what you need. If you use your imagination, many items can be substituted for what you have on hand, can get for free, etc. For example, you may have an abundance of baby food jars from a family toddler. You can easily convert these to be part of a project. Teaching is also about being resourceful. Have family, friends, students and yourself save:

- Baby food jars

- Toilet paper rolls

- Paper towel rolls

- Scraps of material

- Extra tile

- Extra pieces from home improvement projects

- Coffee cans

- Oatmeal containers

- 2 liter bottles

- Cereal boxes

- Egg carton

- Milk jugs

- Salt containers

- Anything you can think of to be re-purposed for a learning tool

Other places to get materials include:

- Home improvement stores (Lowes or Home Depot)

- Dollar Stores

- Educational Supply Stores

- Grocery Store

- Party Supply Store

- Online Resources:

  — Oriental Trading Company: www.orientaltrading.com

  — http://www.etacuisenaire.com

  — Many great songs and activities are available from http://www.newbridgeonline.com/, which is where you can find the MacMillan Sing and Learn songs and other activities. Use the search function and type in "songs for learning". You may also be able to find these used online at www.alibris.com, www.amazon.com, or www.abebooks.com.

www.ingramcontent.com/pod-product-compliance
Lightning Source LLC
LaVergne TN
LVHW081320060426
835509LV00015B/1614